JESUS OF NAZARETH

D0171112

Teacher and Prophet
by Ramsay M. Harik

Forbush Memorial Library
118 MAIN STREET P.O. BOX 468
WESTMINSTER, MA 01473-0468

A Book Report Biography
FRANKLIN WATTS
A Division of Grolier Publishing
New York / London / Hong Kong / Sydney
Danbury, Connecticut

For my parents, Iliya and Elsa Harik

Cover and frontispiece depiction of Jesus by
Anthony Van Dyck (1599–1641)

The author thanks the following, all of whom have generously
contributed their time and talents to this effort: Reverend Byron Bangert,
Professor David Brakke, Elsa and Iliya Harik, Professor Jim Hart,
Professor Luke Johnson, Mary Powell, Bishop John Shelby Spong,
and my editor at Franklin Watts, Lorna Greenberg.

Maps by XNR Productions

Cover photograph ©: SuperStock/Dusseldorf Museum, Germany.

Photographs ©: Archive Photos: 62 (Popperfoto), 43, 45 center, 95; Art
Resource, NY/Erich Lessing: 45 top; Bridgeman Art Library International
Ltd., London/New York: 88 (BAL29580, "Christ Driving the Traders from
the Temple", c.1600. Oil on canvas, by Greco, El (Domenico Theotocopuli).
National Gallery, London, UK); Corbis-Bettmann: 33, 68; Liaison Agency,
Inc./Hulton Getty: 19, 25, 45 bottom; Mary Evans Picture Library: 100;
North Wind Picture Archives: 9, 21, 41, 103; Stock Montage, Inc.: 14, 37,
56, 98; SuperStock, Inc.: 108 (A.K.G., Berlin), 2 (Dusseldorf Museum,
Germany), 65 (Musee des Beaux-Arts, France/The Art Archive), 112
(Staatsgalerie Stuttgart, Germany), 76, 83; The Art Archive: 74.

Visit Franklin Watts on the Internet at:
http://publishing.grolier.com

Library of Congress Cataloging-in-Publication Data

Harik, Ramsay M.
    Jesus of Nazareth : teacher and prophet / by Ramsay M. Harik
        p. cm.—(Book report biography)
    Includes bibliographical references and index.
    ISBN: 0-531-20370-0 (lib. bdg.)   0-531-15552-8 (pbk.)
    1. Jesus Christ—Biography—Juvenile literature. [1. Jesus Christ—
Biography.] I. Title. II. Series.

BT302 .H25 2001
232.9'01—dc21
[B]

© 2001 by Ramsay M. Harik
All rights reserved. Published simultaneously in Canada
Printed in the United States of America
1 2 3 4 5 6 7 8 9 10 R 10 09 08 07 06 05 04 03 02 01

CONTENTS

A MYSTERIOUS LIFE

It is a story familiar to many. Two thousand years ago, in a remote area of the Roman Empire, a boy was born to peasant parents. As he grew up, he learned his father's trade and studied his people's sacred writings. Later, he wandered the country-side, teaching about God and how to lead a good life. In his early thirties, he was arrested by authorities, tortured, and executed. Today, nearly 2 billion people—a third of the world's popula-tion—call themselves followers of this man.

This man was Jesus of Nazareth. But who was he really? What was special about his teach-ings? Why was he executed? Why do so many peo-ple around the globe believe in him as their savior? These are questions that many people have devoted their lives to answering. They are also questions on which people have disagreed strongly—even violently—since the time of Jesus.

A NOTE ABOUT THE BIBLE

What we call "the Bible" is actually the collection of many different sacred scriptures used by both Jews and Christians. The Old Testament (a better term is the Hebrew Scriptures) is the story of the Jewish people and their practices and beliefs. The New Testament (or Christian Scriptures) is the story of the life of Jesus and the development of Christian practices and beliefs. Because Jesus was a Jew and based his life and teachings on the Hebrew Scriptures, both the Hebrew Scriptures and the New Testament are considered holy by Christians.

Every "book" of the Bible is divided into chapters, and each chapter into verses. When the Bible is quoted, a chapter-and-verse citation is given, so that the quotation can be found easily. For instance, "Luke 13:22" means the Gospel of Luke, chapter thirteen, verse twenty-two. This verse reads: "Jesus went through one town and village after another, teaching as he made his way to Jerusalem."

The Bible has been translated from its original Hebrew and Greek into virtually every language on earth. Many translations have been made into English. The most famous, the King James Version, was made in 1611. The elegance and familiarity of this translation make it a favorite among many English-speaking Christians. Yet advances in biblical scholarship and in our understanding of ancient languages have led to newer, more accurate translations. The translation used by most biblical scholars today is the New Revised Standard Version, and it is the source for all Bible quotations in this book.

To explore these questions, we must travel back in time to the land of Galilee, where Jesus grew up. Two thousand years ago, we would see a ruggedly beautiful region, with tiny villages and a few small but growing cities. It was a land of farmers, fishermen, shepherds, and wandering holy men. In the cities of Tiberias and Sepphoris, we also would see shopkeepers, wealthy landowners, tax collectors, and Roman soldiers.

The people of rural Galilee were as rugged and indomitable as the countryside. The presence of a Roman occupation force was intolerable—as was the economic situation. Heavy Roman taxes, along with the taking of their ancestral lands by powerful officials and landlords, were a great bur-

The land of Galilee

den. A growing number of Galileans found themselves landless, poor, and despised.

Beneath the peaceful surface, then, people were stirring. The most hotheaded were gathering weapons, whispering of revolution. Priests and holy men were talking about a great liberator to come, a "Messiah." All the while, heavily armed troops were arriving from Rome.

Into this charged scene, a son was born to a young woman, perhaps only fourteen years old. The New Testament tells us her name was Mary, and that she and her husband Joseph named the baby Jeshua, which in Aramaic means "God saves." Jeshua, or "Jesus" in the Greek language of the New Testament, was their first son. In the culture of Mary and Joseph, as in many cultures in the Mediterranean region even today, the first son is special.

WHAT WAS ARAMAIC?

Several languages were spoken in Galilee. Roman soldiers and officials spoke Latin, upper-class city dwellers and traders spoke Greek, priests spoke the sacred language of Hebrew, and the common folk, like Jesus' family, spoke Aramaic. Aramaic belongs to the Semitic language family, a cousin of the Hebrew and Arabic languages spoken today. But Aramaic as a spoken language has all but died out. Now the language of Jesus is heard only in services of the Maronite Church (based in Lebanon and Syria) and in one or two Syrian villages.

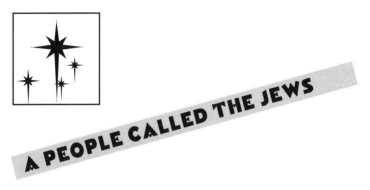

CHAPTER ONE

A PEOPLE CALLED THE JEWS

What was Jesus' culture? Who were his people? Joseph, Mary, and Jesus were Jews, along with the majority of Galilee's population. The homeland of the Jewish people was then known as Palestine, and it included the regions of Judea, Galilee, and Samaria. A tiny sliver of land on the eastern end of the Mediterranean Sea, Palestine had been home to the Jews (earlier known as the Hebrews) for almost two thousand years. Because Jesus lived and died a Jew, we must know who the ancient Jews were and what they believed, if we hope to understand Jesus' life and teachings.

At the time of Jesus' birth, the Jews already had a long history. It began around 1800 B.C.E., according to the Hebrew Scriptures. Abraham, their first great leader, and his tribe, the Hebrews, had come to believe in one God alone—"Yahweh." This put them in opposition to neighboring tribes,

A NOTE ON DATES

Until recently, B.C. was used for the period before the birth of Jesus and A.D. for the period after. This way of dividing historical time into "before Jesus" and "after Jesus" was created by Exiguus, a sixth-century Christian monk. However, he miscalculated and put Jesus' birth (year 0) four to six years too late.

Today's historians no longer use B.C. (Before Christ) and A.D. (Anno Domini, the year of our Lord). As not all the world marks time by Jesus' birth, historians now use B.C.E. (Before the Common Era) and C.E. (Common Era). Today, with better historical records, we know that Jesus was most likely born between 6 and 4 B.C.E.

who believed in many gods. Abraham and the Hebrews left Mesopotamia and settled in Canaan, later called Palestine or "the Holy Land."

Several hundred years later, the scriptures relate, the Hebrews were living in Egypt under a harsh pharaoh. A leader named Moses led them from Egypt back to their homeland. This escape, the "Exodus," is remembered every spring in the holiday of Passover. Resettling in Canaan (often in conflict with the native Canaanites), the Hebrews formed the twelve tribes of Israel, bound together by a common religion.

Under King David and his son Solomon, the twelve tribes were united in 1000 B.C.E. into a powerful kingdom with Jerusalem as capital. For eighty years, the Kingdom of Israel flourished.

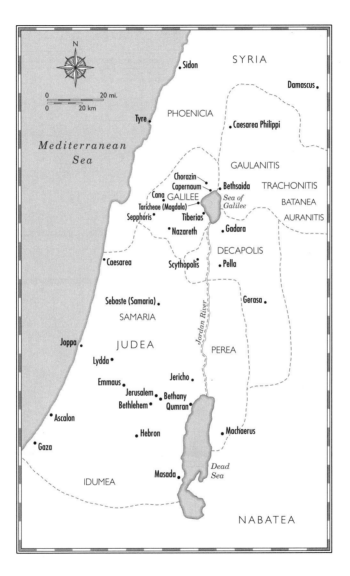

Palestine in the Time of Jesus

The patriarch, Abraham, led his family out of Mesopotamia to settle in Canaan.

Solomon's great temple was built during this "Golden Age." Yet despite his reputation for wisdom, Solomon built his temple with heavy taxes and forced labor. This harsh treatment led to revolt, civil war, and a North–South split in the kingdom.

The two kingdoms, weakened by division, were now easy prey for their larger neighbors. A succession of invaders dominated them for the next thousand years—first Assyrians and Babylonians, then Persians, Greeks, and, finally, Romans.

Remarkably, through this long and troubled history, Abraham's religion developed into one of the world's great religions—Judaism. According to Abraham and Jewish religious leaders ever since, God chose the Hebrews as his special people. He promised to love and protect them so long as they worshiped him alone. They had to give up idol worship and follow his commandments, said to have been revealed to Moses during the long exodus back to the Promised Land.

These commandments are a code of laws designed to ensure a stable society and allegiance to God. They remain at the heart of Jewish religious life, a part of the Hebrew Scriptures called the Torah (the Law). Best known are the ten commandments, but there are 613 laws listed in the Torah, some of which are more relevant today than others. Many deal with daily life, such as how to prepare food or whom one could marry.

Others deal with religious duties: how to make sacrifices to God and how to purify oneself before worship. Others establish a moral code: how to behave toward one another and how to maintain a society of justice and peace.

THE PROPHETS

This concern for the poor and a yearning for peace distinguished the Jewish value system from that of their neighbors. It also stirred the consciences of a special class of Jewish holy men called prophets. The prophets were troubled by the ways the Jewish rulers and people had fallen short of God's demands. Feeling themselves called by God, the prophets denounced injustice, and called their fellow Jews back to God's commandments.

The eighth century B.C.E. prophet Micah cried out, "Alas for those who devise wickedness. . . they covet fields and seize them; houses, and take them away; they oppress householder and house, people and their inheritance." (Micah 2:1–2) He was reminding people that cheating the poor violated God's will as expressed in the Torah. Often, prophets predicted disaster unless the Jews returned to obedience to God and proper dealings with one another. At other times, more optimistic prophets saw a glorious, peace-filled future for the Jewish people when as Micah predicted "they shall beat their swords into plowshares, and their spears into pruning hooks; nation shall not lift up sword against nation, neither shall they learn war any more." (Micah 4:3)

Naturally, the prophets were not always popular with those who did not wish to change their ways. Yet the prophets helped keep alive the Jewish concern for the helpless, through difficult times when people were tempted to think only of themselves. By the time of Jesus, the prophets had been crying out for reform and righteousness for almost a thousand years.

THE MESSIAH

In Jesus' day, another important Jewish belief was in the "Messiah." The word originally meant "anointed one," referring to a ruler such as King David. When a person assumed the throne, a priest anointed the ruler's head with oil to show the ruler's leadership role. Over time, the term came to mean a great liberator, sent by God to establish God's kingdom on earth for the Jews. It would be a shining new kingdom, free of foreign rule, returning the Jews to the glories of the Golden Age of David and Solomon. The prophet Isaiah, speaking for God, described it:

> For I am about to create new heavens and a new earth; the former things shall not be remembered or come to mind. But be glad

and rejoice forever in what I am creating, for I am about to create Jerusalem as a joy and its people as a delight . . . no more shall the sound of weeping be heard in it, or the cry of distress . . . they shall not labor in vain or bear children for calamity; for they shall be offspring blessed by the Lord—and their descendents as well. (Isaiah 65:17–23)

Through the many centuries of suffering, the Jews began to yearn deeply for this new leader to return Israel to its glory. By early in the first century C.E., after decades of harsh Roman rule, many Jews thought the time was ripe for "the anointed one" to appear and banish the oppressors. Looking back at the predictions of the prophets, many Jews believed that God's promise of a new age was about to be fulfilled. Excitement was building among the Jews of Palestine.

The Romans thought otherwise. They liked things as they were. Their armies were in control and their officials were becoming wealthy from heavy taxes on the people. They had little interest in the Jewish religion. They feared a Jewish liberator. In fact, in 4 B.C.E., they brutally put down a Jewish revolt, crucifying two thousand rebels outside the walls of Jerusalem.

Yet angry Jews were determined to rid their homeland of the hated invaders. Many would-be

The Roman rulers of Palestine governed the people, collected taxes, and imposed their own way of life. In Caesaria, the center of Roman rule, they built a great amphitheater for chariot races and gladiator battles.

"Messiahs" were appearing on the streets of Jerusalem, claiming to be the one that God had sent to deliver the Jews. This presented a problem: The people wanted to believe in a Messiah, but which one? What would he look like? How would he act? Would he deliver them from the Romans single-handedly, or would they be expected to fight at his side? How would they know?

CHAPTER TWO

WHAT DO WE KNOW ABOUT JESUS?

Twenty centuries later, those troubled times in Palestine continue to capture our imagination and raise questions. The questions today revolve around the figure of Jesus, whose short life began a revolution in the history of religion. Jesus has been the object of reverence and debate. What is it about this first-century Jewish teacher that inspires such wonder and such controversy?

One obvious answer is that for many, Jesus is not simply a man who lived and died like other men and women. For Christians through the ages, he has been a divine savior sent to rescue believers from the snares of sin and death. How this complicated set of beliefs began is an interesting story, but not the focus of this book. The point here is that the Jesus of belief, however real for Christians, lives apart from the historian's tools. Historians and biographers, seeking to learn what they can about the man named Jesus, must put aside religious *beliefs about* Jesus and instead look for historical *evidence of* Jesus.

A HOPELESS TASK?

When we try to do this, we run into troubling roadblocks. What real evidence is there? What do

The Mount of Olives and the Garden of Gethsemane, where Jesus is believed to have rested

we really know about Jesus, and how do we know it? It turns out that we know very little. It has been two thousand years, after all, and historical records about Jesus are few. Jesus himself left no writings, and the earliest records were written decades after his death. Moreover, these accounts are not always historically accurate, and they leave out a great deal we would like to know. What did Jesus look like? Who taught him and what did he study? What were his hopes and dreams? About these and many other questions we can only wonder.

What do we really know about Jesus?

Perhaps if we had more reliable historical information, it would be easier to agree about the details and importance of Jesus' life. Because we have so little, people tend to create a Jesus who fits their idea of what he should be. Further, a few scholars question whether he existed at all! Perhaps the only thing the experts agree on is that we will never have an accurate record of Jesus' life, nor one that satisfies everybody.

But isn't it enough that we have the Bible? Don't the Gospel stories in the first four books of the Christian Scriptures (the New Testament) tell us all we need to know? Unfortunately, it's not so simple. While these stories are powerful presentations of the life of Jesus and of his importance for believers, they are not strictly accurate historical biographies. We will explore the reasons for this in Chapter 3.

SIFTING THE CLUES

Nonetheless, an attempt to understand the historical Jesus is not hopeless. Biblical scholars, trained in the history, languages, and writings of ancient Palestine, are discovering new clues and achieving new insights about the world in which Jesus lived. From these discoveries, they hope to get a better idea of how he lived, what motivated him, and what impact he had on people. Today is an exciting time to study the historical Jesus. We have more information and a better understanding of his life and his world than ever before. any time. And the steady stream of books and documentaries about Jesus reveal that the public today is keenly interested in what the scholars discover.

What these scholars are doing can be seen as detective work, with the life of Jesus as the mystery. They examine the scanty evidence and search for clues, from historical records, archeological evidence, and the Gospels. Then they painstakingly try to piece together a story that makes sense. Their goal is to arrive not at certainty, but at the best possible guesses. It is tricky work—controversial and exciting.

HISTORICAL RECORDS

Historical records give us valuable information about what was happening in Palestine before, during, and after the life of Jesus. Especially useful are the writings of the Jewish historian Josephus. In the late first century, Josephus recorded in detail the dramatic events that took place in first-century Palestine. He included descriptions of the daily life and religious practices of the Jews, and a great deal about the Roman occupation of Palestine.

The Romans were originally a tribe in what is today Italy. Through military might and effective administration of conquered lands, by Jesus' time they ruled the entire Mediterranean region and beyond. Wherever they went, they brought engineering skills and new ideas and culture, and the brutal suppression of any resistance.

The Romans conquered Palestine in 63 B.C.E. Some time later, they allowed a local leader, Herod the Great, to rule for them. So long as Herod kept order and respected the Romans' authority (which included collecting taxes to send to Rome), the Romans were content. When Herod died in 4 B.C.E., however, confusion and rebellion reigned, and the Romans decided to establish more direct rule in Palestine.

They divided Palestine into several provinces, including Judea (from which we get the words

The works of Josephus, (37–100 C.E.) are an important source of information about ancient Palestine.

Judaism and *Jew*) and Galilee. In Judea, they placed a Roman governor, known as a procurator. From 26 to 36 C.E., this position was held by Pontius Pilate. Galilee was run by one of Herod's sons, Herod Antipas. Roman soldiers enforced order throughout Palestine. While some Jews profited from their dealings with the Romans, most suffered. Heavy tax burdens oppressed nearly every-one, and many people were forced to forfeit their lands. The constant presence of Roman soldiers, and their contempt for the Jewish religion, offend-ed the proud Jews of Judea and Galilee. This, then, was the unhappy political situation in which Jesus grew up.

ARCHEOLOGICAL EVIDENCE

What can a few pieces of ancient pottery, the charred foundation of a stone building, and a Roman mosaic tell us about the life of Jesus? As it turns out, quite a bit. Just as historical records tell us about the political and religious situation, archeological evidence—the physical remains uncovered from earlier times—reveals something about the cultural influences in Jesus' world.

The excavations at the Greek city of Seppho-ris in Galilee are an example. Traditionally, Christians and Bible scholars have imagined Jesus growing up in a remote village setting. From recent digs at Sepphoris, we see that only four miles (6.4 km) from his birthplace of Nazareth, within walking distance, was a bustling, multicultural city of perhaps 40,000 peo-ple. It is hard to imagine Jesus in quite the same way now, knowing that he grew up only two hours' walk from this city, a city growing so quickly that

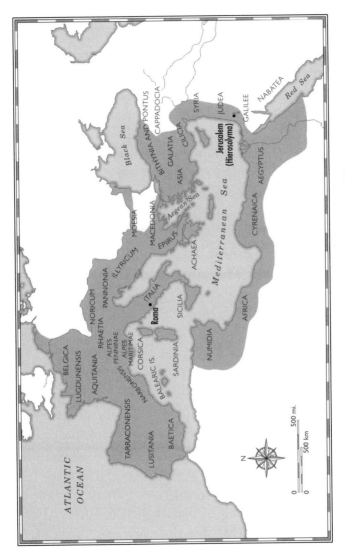

ATLANTIC OCEAN

LUSITANIA
BAETICA
TARRACONENSIS
NARBONENSIS
BALEARIC IS.
AQUITANIA
LUGDUNENSIS
BELGICA
ALPES MARITIMAE
ALPES PENNINAE
RHAETIA
NORICUM
PANNONIA
ILLYRICUM
MOESIA

CORSICA
SARDINIA
SICILIA
ITALIA
Roma
NUMIDIA
AFRICA

Mediterranean Sea

MACEDONIA
EPIRUS
ACHAEA
Aegean Sea
ASIA
GALATIA
BITHYNIA AND PONTUS
CAPPADOCIA
CILICIA
SYRIA

Black Sea

JUDEA
GALILEE
Jerusalem (Hierosolyma)
NABATEA
Red Sea
CYRENAICA
AEGYPTUS

N

0   500 mi.
0   500 km

The Roman Empire in the Time of Jesus

it probably drew skilled workers like Jesus from surrounding villages.

What he might have seen there and what ideas he might have absorbed we can only imagine, but a key clue is the word *Greek*. Why, if Palestine was a Jewish land, and if it was occupied by the Romans, was Sepphoris known as a *Greek* city? Archeological digs such as that at Sepphoris, with discoveries of artwork, building styles, and objects used in daily life, reveal an answer to that question.

In important cities around the Mediterranean, people of all ethnic backgrounds often imitated Greek culture. The prestige of the Greek civilization, and the spread of that civilization as far east as India by Alexander the Great and his armies in the fourth century B.C.E., established Greek culture as the culture of choice. Even the Romans imitated the Greeks, and many urban Jews, especially those scattered outside of Palestine, enjoyed Greek culture. Citizens of cities such as Sepphoris spoke Greek, saw Greek plays, exercised in Greek gymnasiums, and bantered about Greek philosophy.

Again, this is a world we do not ordinarily associate with Jesus. Yet it seems likely that he was exposed to this eye-opening mix of styles and ideas. Many scholars now think that Jesus' ideas and teachings were influenced not only by his own

Jewish culture but by Greek attitudes and philosophy as well.

THE GOSPELS

Our third and most important source of clues is the Gospels—the first four books of the Christian Scriptures (New Testament). The Gospels are a form of biography written by followers of Jesus. Yet they were written with a purpose other than just recounting the historical facts. The Gospels were the writers' attempts to share their wonder at Jesus' life, and to convince readers to join them in worshiping Jesus as their Lord. They focus on his wondrous deeds and inspiring teachings. They give special attention to his death and mysterious resurrection, so full of meaning for Christians. The Gospels are like a series of shining portraits, each giving us insight into this man as the faith-filled gospel writers saw him.

Many stories about Jesus' life were written in the decades after his death, some more reliable than others. Four were chosen by Christian leaders in the early third century as being the closest to the authentic words and deeds of Jesus. These four are known as the Gospels of Matthew, Mark, Luke, and John, and together they make up the heart of the Christian Scriptures (New Testament). Others, such as the Gospel of Thomas and the Gospel of the Nazoreans, were rejected by early Church leaders as different from the "official" view of Jesus. Yet today, these extra sources help scholars understand the diversity of views held by early Christians.

The Gospel writers wrote passionately and with insight. Yet most likely, they did not themselves know Jesus. They were writing forty to seventy years after his death, basing their accounts on memories passed down from believer to believer. Furthermore, each Gospel writer saw Jesus in his own particular way. It is not surprising, then, that the accounts often differ.

Most biblical scholars acknowledge that the Gospels contain a mix of accurate memories, distorted and hazy memories, and stories created or expanded by the writers. In doing this, the writers were not being deceitful. It was a Jewish tradition to explain the present in terms of what the sacred scriptures told of the past. The Gospel writers were Jews and tried to explain the life of this mysterious Jesus by searching the old Hebrew Scriptures for clues. They made connections between Jesus and the heroes of the Jewish past, such as Moses and Joshua. They pictured Jesus saying and doing amazing things that showed him to be a worthy successor to these heroes. Then, they hoped, their readers would see that Jesus was indeed the one predicted by the prophets, the Messiah who had come to save the world.

The job of biblical scholars is to tease apart the portions of the Gospels that are historical from those that come from the writers' imaginations. Rather than throwing out the Gospels as unreliable, most scholars find in them a vivid picture of the historical Jesus, a rich source of details about his life.

We have little else to go on. Apart from a few brief mentions of Jesus by non-Christian writers, which we will examine later, the Gospels are the only written information about Jesus from that time period. This is why, for all their problems, the Gospels are our best source for reconstructing the life of Jesus.

The stage is now set. With historical and archeological clues, we can begin to imagine Jesus' world. With a careful selection of the stories in the Gospels, we can picture the crucial events and teachings of his career. It is time now to piece together a life of Jesus.

CHAPTER THREE

JESUS' EARLY YEARS

The Gospel accounts of Jesus' birth contain some of the most beautiful writing in the Bible. The Gospel of Luke with its awe-stricken shepherds, worshipful kings, and heralding angels, captures the imagination. This miraculous birth, set in Bethlehem, city of David, seems full of promise. Yet most likely, Jesus' birth and early days were like those of any other Galilean baby.

How to explain, then, the beautiful birth stories in the Bible? It seems they reflect less historical fact than the Gospel writers' desire to show Jesus in a special light. Throughout the ancient world, heroes, religious figures, and even pharaohs and emperors were often seen as having miraculous births and a special connection to the gods. Biblical scholars tell us that the Gospel writers were probably following this common practice. It is also unlikely that any records of a peasant birth

The birth of Jesus, as portrayed by Martin Schongauer, a fifteenth-century German artist

would have been made. The Gospel writers probably had no real information, and so they filled in the gap with birth legends that had been passed down from earlier Christians. These Christians, like the Gospel writers, used their imaginations and the Hebrew Scriptures to shape stories about Jesus that "proved" he was the Messiah.

One fairly reliable clue about Jesus' birth comes in the Gospels of Matthew and Luke. They tell us that Jesus was born near the end of Herod the Great's reign. Herod died in 4 B.C.E., so Jesus was probably born in 5 or 4 B.C.E. As to the site, many scholars feel that he was probably born in Nazareth, not Bethlehem. The Gospel writers were moved to portray Bethlehem as Jesus' birthplace because ancient prophecies predicted that the savior would come from Bethlehem, the city of David. If he was born in Nazareth, it would be harder for the Gospel writers to convince readers that he was the Messiah.

GROWING UP

We can be fairly certain of where Jesus grew up, for the Gospels consistently tell us that he came from the Galilean hill town of Nazareth. What was life like for the young Jesus? Again, we can only make some educated guesses. Apart from one story in the Gospel of Luke, the Bible contains no accounts of Jesus between his birth and the age of

PROPHECY

In their role as critics of Israelite society, the prophets made predictions based on how people behaved. Their message was usually quite simple: If you continue in your wicked ways, God will punish the whole nation. If you act with charity and righteousness, God will establish a shining new Israel of peace and prosperity.

Several prophets spoke of a Messiah who would lead the people into this new age. These lines from the eighth century B.C.E. prophet Isaiah are a famous example:

> For a child has been born for us, a son given to us;
> Authority rests upon his shoulders;
> And he is named "Wonderful Counselor,
> Mighty God, Everlasting Father, Prince of Peace."
> (Isaiah 9:6–7)

Reading centuries-old scriptures like these, the Gospel writers felt sure that Jesus was the fulfillment of the prophets' predictions.

about thirty. Yet since we know quite a bit about life in towns like first-century Nazareth, we can imagine something of how Jesus spent his early years. We know, for instance, that as the son of a craftsman (perhaps a carpenter, though the Greek word in the Gospels could mean any skilled worker or artisan), Jesus would be expected to learn his father's trade.

We also know that he probably would have gone to school from roughly age six to at least twelve or thirteen. Schooling was unusual in the ancient world, but the Jews valued learning highly, and so school was generally available for all boys, rich and poor alike. (In Palestine, as in most of the world at that time, girls were expected to work at home; educating them was considered a waste of time.) School for the Jews revolved around the Torah. Learning to read meant learning the Hebrew Scriptures, eventually memorizing much of the Law, along with the Jewish prayers and history. Students gathered in the local place of worship, a synagogue, and learned from a religious teacher, a priest, or a scribe.

Jesus would have gathered with his neighbors at the synagogue every week for Shabbat prayers. Shabbat, the Sabbath, was the Jewish day of rest and worship, prescribed in God's commandments. Then, as today, it extended from sundown on Friday to sundown on Saturday. But religion filled the lives of the ancient Jews every day, and in many ways. The young Jesus was surely steeped in the great stories and rich spiritual wisdom of his people.

What else can scholars tell us about the young Jesus? Very little. But one story in the Gospel of Luke gives some insight into the mind and spirit of the boy as he approached manhood.

"LOST" IN THE TEMPLE

Luke was a well-educated, Greek-speaking Christian who wrote about Jesus sometime around 80

The scene of Jesus speaking with the teachers in the temple is based on a painting by Heinrich J.M.F. Hoffman, a nineteenth-century German artist.

or 90 C.E. In this passage, Luke recounts a story about a boy with some unusual gifts:

> Now every year his parents went to Jerusalem for the festival of the Passover. And when he was twelve years old, they went up as usual for the festival. When the festival was ended and they started to return, the boy Jesus stayed behind in Jerusalem, but his parents did not know it.

▲ 37 ▲

Assuming that he was in the group of travelers, they went for a day's journey. Then they started to look for him among their relatives and friends. When they did not find him, they returned to Jerusalem to search for him. After three days they found him in the temple, sitting among the teachers, listening to them and asking them questions. And all who heard him were amazed at his understanding and his answers. . . . Then he went down with them and came to Nazareth, and was obedient to them. His mother treasured all these things in her heart. And Jesus increased in wisdom and in years, and in divine and human favor. (Luke 2:41–47, 51–52)

This story expresses the religious sensitivity and awareness that Jesus showed even at the age of twelve. He had so excelled in his studies and in his religious growth that he could converse with the learned Jewish teachers known as rabbis.

According to Luke, Jesus "increased in wisdom" as he grew to manhood. It is not hard to imagine a young man with Jesus' gifts gaining wisdom and understanding in ancient Galilee. He would have learned about

Jesus "increased in wisdom"

hard work and obedience from his parents, about the forces of life and death from the shepherds and farmers, about the love of God from his teachers in the synagogue, and about the glories of God's creation in his wanderings through the rugged countryside.

These sources of inspiration show up again and again in his later teachings. Other sources contributed to his mental and spiritual formation as well. His encounters with the mix of Greek, Roman, and Jewish ideas in the nearby cities must have stimulated his thinking about the world and its ways. New ideas about religion and philosophy, carried by caravan traders passing through town from far-off Egypt and Persia, no doubt captured his attention. Add to this his sensitivity to his people's suffering under the Romans, and we have the ingredients for his later passionate teachings and actions.

CHAPTER FOUR

A MAN WITH A MISSION

From Jesus at twelve, we jump ahead to Jesus at thirty, for nowhere in the four Gospels do we find accounts of what he was doing in the years between. Perhaps he traveled to some of the strange lands he had heard tales of, or perhaps he spent time living with some of the Jewish communities in Palestine devoted to a life of holiness. At thirty, however, the story of Jesus explodes upon the pages of the Bible. Whatever he had been doing in his teens and twenties, he was now ready to begin what is known as his "public ministry." First, however, came an encounter with John.

JOHN THE BAPTIST

John the Baptist, according to Luke, was a distant cousin of Jesus, of about the same age. He was a strong and fiery man, passionate about his Jewish religion. People gathered from miles around to hear him preach on the arid banks of the lower Jordan River near the Dead Sea. Many considered him a prophet, and it seems he had a large following by the time Jesus came to see him.

John is one of the most colorful characters in the Bible. Josephus praised him for his "eloquence that had so great an effect" on people. To under-

John the Baptist, preaching in the wilderness

THE TEMPLE

The temple in Jerusalem was the Jews' holiest site. Built by Herod the Great and his successors in the first century C.E., the temple complex sat on the ruins of Solomon's temple, destroyed by the Babylonians in 587 B.C.E. Larger than twenty football fields, the temple complex was an architectural marvel.

For Jews throughout the Mediterranean region, the temple was their center of worship. On pilgrimage feasts such as Passover, thousands would come to bring their sacrifices to God. Hundreds of priests carried out the slaughter and burning of pigeons, goats, cows, and lambs, brought or purchased by the pilgrims. The temple was also a setting for religious teaching and discussion, for private prayer, and for the administration of temple finances and policies by the high priest and his staff.

The temple was a source of pride for the Jews—and of controversy. Many were scandalized by the statues and ornamentation that defied the Jewish commandment against "graven images." Some resented what they saw as cooperation between the chief priests and the hated Romans. Others objected to the heavy taxes imposed to help pay for the temple's construction and maintenance. Still others considered the priests corrupt and unqualified for their holy tasks. Evidently, Jesus shared some of

stand what John was doing on the banks of the Jordan, and why he was so popular, we must look at the state of the Jewish religion at the time.

Just as today there are many ways of being a Christian (or a Jew, Muslim, or Buddhist), there were many ways of being a Jew in first-century these objections, for the Gospels describe his protest there, known as "the cleansing of the temple."

Controversy swirled around the temple until its destruction by the Romans in 70 C.E. The eyewitness Josephus described the horror: "The temple hill, enveloped in flames from top to bottom, appeared to be boiling up from its very roots; yet the sea of flame was nothing [compared] to the ocean of blood." All that remains of Herod's great temple is its western wall, a holy site for Jews today.

Palestine. Some Jews were content with making the temple sacrifices that had been part of Jewish worship from before the time of Solomon. These Jews were often from the priestly caste, which enjoyed power and prosperity from its connection with the temple. Many Jews, however, felt excluded from the blessings of the temple. Other Jews, especially those living in regions distant from Jerusalem, such as Galilee and Samaria, practiced local variations of Judaism that the "Temple Jews" of Judea looked down upon. And then there were the Essenes.

THE ESSENES AND JOHN

The Essenes were one of the various Jewish sects that made first-century Judaism a diverse and complex religion. Beginning in the second century B.C.E., they decided that the situation at the Jerusalem temple was wrong. The priests were "corrupt," they were from the "wrong" families, they conducted the sacrifices in the "wrong" ways. Convinced of their own righteousness, the Essenes separated themselves from Jerusalem. In the Judean desert, they could live a life of holy purity far from the city's corruption.

In the late 1940s, a great archeological find revealed how extreme these Essenes were. The Dead Sea Scrolls, discovered in desert caves above the Dead Sea, contain two-thousand-year-old scriptures associated with the Essenes, with titles such as "The War of the Sons of Light Against the Sons of Darkness" and "The Manual of Discipline."

Apparently, the Essenes were preparing for "the end time," the apocalypse. Many Jews of the time believed in an apocalypse, the Day of Judg-

In 1947, ancient scrolls were discovered in desert caves at Qumran (top), near the Dead Sea. The manuscripts were in clay urns (center), and have been studied by archeologists and biblical scholars. The page shown (bottom) is from the Old Testament book of Isaiah.

ment when God would end the suffering of the present evil age and usher in a glorious new creation. Yet the Essenes lived and breathed this expectation. They were convinced that it was coming, that it would be bloody, and that they alone would emerge as the rightful inheritors of God's new kingdom.

What does this have to do with John the Baptist? A number of scholars see connections between John and the Essenes. Whether he was an Essene or not is debated, but living in the Judean wilderness so near their community, he seems to have been influenced by them. Like them, he lived a life apart, a life of purity and simplicity, in expectation of "the end time." His fierce preaching divided the world into the righteous and the evil. Yet unlike them, he wanted to bring righteousness to as many Jews as possible, not just to a chosen few.

This was the heart of John's preaching. He warned people that the evil age was upon them, that God's commandments had been forgotten and God's judgment would be swift and severe. To be saved, they must earn salvation by repenting, and acting with charity toward one another:

And the crowds asked him, "What then should we do?" In reply he said to them, "Whoever has two coats must share with anyone who has none; and whoever has food must do likewise." Even tax collectors came to be baptized, and they asked him, "Teacher, what should we do?" And he said to them, "Collect no more than the amount prescribed for you." Soldiers also asked him, "And we, what should we do?" He said to them, "Do not extort money from anyone by threats or false accusations, and be satisfied with your wages." (Luke 3:10–14)

John's message about God's judgment was harsh, but his ideal of human behavior was of gentleness. Many were moved by the power of his preaching. To show that they were "washing themselves clean" of their sins, they had John baptize them—plunging them into the rushing waters of the Jordan River. Baptism, from a Greek word meaning "dipping," was practiced in various ritual forms in the Judaism of the time. The baptism practiced by John was particularly powerful, an experience of sudden conversion into the holy life to which John called his fellow Jews.

Jesus was one of those who traveled through the desert to the banks of the Jordan to hear John preach. According to one Gospel, Jesus spent several days in the desert with John. Perhaps for a time he was a disciple, a passionate follower of John's teachings. In any case, something in John moved Jesus deeply. He had John baptize him. At this, according to all four Gospels, the Holy Spirit "descended upon" Jesus.

Clearly, this was a powerful moment for Jesus. Most scholars feel that the baptism by John was a real occurrence in Jesus' life. Here

Filled with the power of the Spirit

was a turning point for Jesus, an awakening to God's power within him that left him "filled with the power of the Spirit." (Luke 4:14) He was now almost ready to begin his ministry. Aflame with John's ideals, perhaps mindful of the Essenes' ideas as well, he needed time to arrive at his own understanding of God's mysterious plan.

INTO THE DESERT

In many cultures, spiritual young people set out into the desert or the wilderness for a period of solitary fasting, prayer, and spiritual purification. For the Jews, the desert was an especially meaningful place. It was in the Sinai Desert that the tribe of Hebrews, led by Moses, had been tested for forty years and forged together as a people of God. In a similar way, the Gospels tell us, Jesus entered the Judean desert for forty days of testing and spiritual development.

The Gospels picture this period in the desert as a time of temptations by the devil. Quoting Hebrew Scriptures, Jesus rebuked the devil and remained loyal to God. Though these accounts may be largely fanciful, they present a convincing picture of a changed Jesus. The Jesus who emerged from the desert seemed to have a stronger sense of God's power within himself, and a clearer idea of what he was supposed to do with it.

From the Judean desert, Jesus returned to his homeland in Galilee. Luke reports that he was "about thirty" at the time. In Galilee, he began wandering the countryside, visiting towns and cities, teaching, healing, and maybe also baptizing people himself. Jesus now had his own ministry, his own plan of action. What did he hope to accomplish with his newfound spiritual power, and how did he hope to do it?

"FULFILLING THE SCRIPTURES"

Scholars argue endlessly about these questions, and indeed, there is no way of knowing just what Jesus had in mind as he set out on his mission. Like many spiritual masters, Jesus often spoke in riddles and acted in ways that were not easy to understand. The gospels show that even those closest to Jesus were frequently confused about what he was doing. It's likely, too, that in the two or three years between his baptism and his death, Jesus' own ideas about his mission changed. But a clue about his early sense of mission comes in the Gospel of Luke, as Jesus "announces" himself to his fellow Jews.

It was common for wandering religious teachers to visit and teach in local synagogues. The following episode occurred in the synagogue of the town where Jesus grew up, Nazareth. Opening the Hebrew Scriptures, he read aloud from the Book of the Prophet Isaiah:

> The Spirit of the Lord is upon me, because he has anointed me to bring good news to the poor. He has sent me to proclaim release to the captives and recovery of sight to the blind, to let the oppressed go free, to proclaim the year of the Lord's favor. (Luke 4:18–19)

After the reading, he began to teach, saying, "Today this scripture has been fulfilled in your hearing." These bold words seemed to suggest that Jesus saw himself carrying out the role of the Hebrew prophets before him, preaching "good news to the poor," bringing God's liberating justice to those

"Good news to the poor"

who suffer, and calling his fellow Jews to create a society of justice and fairness for all.

To prove himself as a prophet, he needed help. Bringing a whole nation the good news of God's salvation was a tall order. Like wise men and dynamic religious teachers everywhere, Jesus attracted large crowds as he traveled across Palestine. In time, he collected a small group of followers, known in the Gospels as "the twelve disciples." Jesus taught these disciples to help him bring his message to the people and also perhaps to heal the sick. One of them, Simon (called Peter), came to be known as the leader among them.

WOMEN DISCIPLES?

Along with the twelve male disciples, several women followed Jesus as well. Luke 8:1–3 mentions Mary Magdalene, Joanna, and Susanna among "many others."

For a religious teacher to associate publicly with women, and to travel with them, was a scandal in first-century Palestine. Women were seen as incapable of understanding much about religion. Worse, they were seen as sexually distracting to the teacher, who needed to keep his thoughts on "holy" matters. By inviting women into his circle of friends and disciples, Jesus was offering them a sense of self-worth, and was challenging his society's attitudes toward women. It is not surprising, then, that as the Christian movement developed after Jesus' death, it attracted many women.

Jesus' small band of Jewish disciples moved about the countryside on foot. They lived simply and shared what they had. They probably relied on the generosity of friends, family, and sympathizers, and there are several scenes in the Gospels in which Jesus is invited to meals at peoples' homes. At times they must have slept in the open air as they crisscrossed Palestine. Some of them, such as the fisherman Simon Peter and his brother Andrew, gave up busy livelihoods to follow Jesus. Others, such as Simon the Zealot, may have been political revolutionaries hoping that Jesus would lead them against the Romans. All chose to leave behind home and family in order to be with their master and see where he would lead them.

CHAPTER FIVE

HEALINGS AND MIRACLES

The first century was a time of crisis in Palestine, a time of suffering and confusion. More people were becoming poor and landless, due to the heavy Roman taxes. Sickness and hunger were all around. There was also a spiritual hunger in the people's hearts and minds. As the Romans took firmer control, God's promise of salvation for the Jews seemed further off than ever.

Many felt that their religious leaders—the priests and rabbis—were doing little to answer their fears that God had abandoned them. The people hoped for new answers, new leaders who could reassure them of God's love. Most of all, they were looking for the Messiah and a new kingdom of God. Yet there was great uncertainty about how to recognize this Messiah. All they could do was look for signs of his coming, evidence that he was here and was establishing his kingdom.

A MAN OF COMPASSION

Jesus was keenly aware of his people's suffering and yearning. Again and again in the Gospels, we see him meeting, even seeking out, those who suffered. The Gospels tell us that he was "moved with compassion." The English word compassion comes from Latin roots meaning "to suffer with," and it seems a fitting term for what led Jesus to reach out to those in need. He was one of them; their suffering was the suffering of the whole Jewish nation, and he felt it deeply.

Jesus experienced his God as a God of compassion, a God who feels for and acts on behalf of his suffering creatures. This understanding of God was rooted in the Hebrew Scriptures, especially in the words of the prophets. A repeating theme in the Gospels is Jesus' desire to demonstrate this compassion, to act as he felt his father, God, acts. Jesus' teachings emphasized that this "imitation of God" was not for him alone, but for everyone, so that God's love and compassion could become the model for everybody's behavior.

The love Jesus spoke of was difficult, a love that extended to one's enemies and to the undeserving, not just to friends and family. Only then could the Jews become the community of justice and peace that God intended. In a collection of teachings known as "the Sermon on the Mount,"

Jesus developed this theme. This forgiving love, Jesus claimed, was at the heart of Jewish teaching. Only through selfless love could enemies be reconciled and hardened hearts be softened: "Love your enemies, and do good, and lend, expecting

"Love your enemies, and do good"

nothing in return. Your reward will be great, and you will be children of the Most High; for he is kind to the ungrateful and the wicked. Be merciful, just as your Father is merciful." (Luke 6:35–36)

A HEALER

Jesus tried to show what this love and compassion looked like in real life, and how it could liberate people from suffering. One way he acted on his compassion was through healing the sick and the infirm: "And Jesus went about all the cities and villages, teaching in their synagogues . . . and curing every disease and every sickness. When he saw the crowds, he had compassion for them, because they were harassed and helpless, like sheep without a shepherd." (Matthew 9:35–36)

A person with powers to heal has always attracted attention, especially in the days before modern medicine. Wandering healers were com-

*An engraving by the nineteenth-century
French artist Paul Gustave Doré portrays
Jesus healing the sick.*

mon in Palestine and throughout the ancient world. As word of Jesus' powers spread from village to village, the afflicted flocked to him. According to the Gospels, Jesus often healed with a touch, or a simple word of encouragement. The healing came from the power of God acting through Jesus, as well as from the faith in Jesus demonstrated by those who sought his help.

The modern world tends to be skeptical of this sort of "unscientific" healing, although modern medical science recognizes that some ailments

MIRACLES

The Gospel stories of healing seem to carry authentic memories of Jesus' power. Less reliable are the stories of Jesus' miracles, such as when he walks on water in Mark 6 or raises Lazarus from the dead in John 11. The Gospel writers believed Jesus was the Messiah. Their conviction—and their desire to convince others—would have led them to compare Jesus with earlier Jewish heroes. These heroes were sometimes depicted as possessing miraculous, God-given powers. Indeed, the Hebrew Scriptures are filled with their stories: Moses parting the Red Sea, or the prophet Elisha raising the dead. The Gospel writers wanted to present Jesus as a miracle-worker, too—as evidence that he was the Messiah. Are these stories based on actual events, or are they the Gospel writers' expressions of the divine power that, according to Jewish belief, surged through heroes such as Moses, Elisha, and Jesus? Questions like these show how hard it is to separate the Jesus of faith from the Jesus of history.

do seem to arise from psychological or emotional distress. The healing of these ailments can sometimes occur through the easing of that distress. Certain kinds of deafness, blindness, paralysis, skin diseases, and other ailments may have a psychological base, and these are the types of disorders that Jesus is said to have "cured."

This way of understanding the mind-body connection is quite ancient. Jesus and other healers through the ages have healed not through medicine but by restoring their troubled patients' peace of mind. In Jesus' day, sickness was generally seen as a sign of sinfulness. A sick person was often thought to have been afflicted because he or she had sinned, was "unholy," or was "possessed" by a demon. Healing was sometimes a matter of easing their feelings of guilt or their sense of being an outcast. Whatever the source, Jesus seemed to have the power to restore many of these people to "wholeness" and health. In the process, he also taught them about the power of God's love.

To many witnesses, Jesus' healings were a sign that he was holy. The Gospel writers, especially Mark, saw these powers as "signs of the kingdom," signs that Jesus was the Messiah. But the Gospels were written many decades later. Were Jesus' healings enough to convince the Jews that he was the one who would usher in the kingdom of God?

CHAPTER SIX

"THE KINGDOM OF GOD IS AMONG YOU"

Soon after Jesus began his mission in Galilee, John the Baptist was arrested (and eventually executed) for his fiery criticism of the Galilean ruler Herod Antipas. According to Matthew, the imprisoned John sent a heartfelt question to Jesus: "Are you he who is to come [the Messiah] or are we to wait for another?" And Jesus answered John's messengers, "Go and tell John what you hear and see: the blind receive their sight and the lame walk, lepers are cleansed and the deaf hear, the dead are raised, and the poor have good news brought to them." (Matthew 11:2–5)

Like the story of the synagogue teaching in the Gospel of Luke, this episode holds several clues as we try to sort out who Jesus was and what his mission was. The first clue is in John's question, "Are you he who is to come?" John may have thought that Jesus was the Messiah. Yet in this question we hear some doubt in his voice: "or are we to wait for another?" If Jesus was the Messiah, why hadn't he shown it with superhuman heroics?

Jesus' reply was just as telling. Open your eyes, he said. Look at the great deeds I have done. They are not deeds of political revolution, but isn't it possible that the kingdom of God could come about through acts of healing and comfort? Here we have a hint of how Jesus may have thought about the kingdom of God. Perhaps it was not some paradise off in the future. Perhaps it would not be reached through the violent overthrow of the Romans by a King David-like warrior. Perhaps it was happening now, quietly, under the noses of the Romans. Perhaps the real revolution was happening in people's hearts, inspiring them to treat one another with compassion and forgiveness. And perhaps he, Jesus, was helping it to happen.

TEACHINGS ABOUT THE KINGDOM OF GOD

Jesus' thoughts and actions concerning the kingdom of God are one of the great mysteries in the history of religion. The Hebrew Scriptures expressed the hope of a "Golden Age," but they described it vaguely and in a variety of ways. This led to confusion. Now Jesus was talking about the kingdom of God in a way that confused matters further. What did it mean when he told them the kingdom of God "is like a mustard seed" (Luke 13:19) or "the kingdom of God is among you"? (Luke 17:21)

We don't know which of Jesus' sayings about the kingdom are authentic, and which were added by the Gospel writers. Sometimes Jesus sounded like an Essene or a prophet, warning of a violent "end time." In these sayings, God is an angry judge, and there will be no mistaking his coming:

> the sun will be darkened, and the moon will not give its light, and the stars will be falling from heaven, and the powers in the heavens will be shaken. Then they will see the "Son of Man coming in clouds" with great power and glory. (Mark 13:24–26)

More often, Jesus spoke of the kingdom of God in gentler terms. He asked his hearers to open their eyes, to see what he saw. Wherever God's people realized God's tremendous love and shared that love, the kingdom could take root. The kingdom was not a kingdom in the usual sense, but rather a society in which people's hearts were ruled by God alone. It could even take shape under Roman domination. People may not be able to change their earthly rulers, but they could enjoy the freedom and community that comes from living in

Jesus traveled about, describing the kingdom of God.

God's love. The power of that love was such that ultimately it could transform even the Romans.

This kingdom of God, then, arrived not with a bang, but with a thousand subtle signs of God's increasing presence in people's lives. And it was happening now, Jesus claimed. "The kingdom of God is not coming with things that can be observed; nor will they say, 'Look, here it is!' or 'There it is!' For, in fact, the kingdom of God is among you." (Luke 17:21) One "enters" the kingdom of God not by political revolt, but "like a child," accepting God's love and loving one another.

"The kingdom of God is among you."

Many scholars feel that Jesus' ideas of the kingdom may have combined both views. Like John and earlier prophets, Jesus had faith in God's plan for the Jewish people. He may have feared that unless his society repented, disaster would befall the Jews. But unlike earlier prophets, he seemed to see the kingdom unfolding not in the future, but in the present, everywhere around him: in the healings, in people's yearning for a more God-filled life, in the tiny "mustard seeds" of faith that were taking root and turning lives into "trees" of love, joy, and salvation.

Whatever Jesus meant by "the kingdom of God," it is clear from the Gospels that this passionate vision drove his ministry. His teachings and actions flowed out of this idea that the kingdom of God was available to all who would listen. In a time when many Jews were unsure of God's plan, Jesus' message must have inspired hope.

A SOURCE OF HOPE

What was it about Jesus that attracted so many? Beyond their belief in his power to heal, the answer may be the acceptance and hope that he offered those who needed it most. The poor, the sick, and despised outcasts all felt rejected by their society and by God. Jesus drew them in and assured them that God did love them. He showed them that love and taught them to love each other. He offered sinners a way out of their shame, a path of repentance leading to self-respect and joy. He preached God's compassion, and taught that God would judge them less on their past deeds than on the compassion they showed one another: "Do not judge, and you will not be judged; do not condemn, and you will not be condemned. Forgive, and you will be forgiven. . . ." (Luke 6:37–38).

The story of the adulterous woman is an example of Jesus' message of the power of forgiveness and the possibility of new life. Some religious leaders had caught a woman in a sexual sin and claimed that the law demanded that she be stoned. They asked Jesus his opinion, and he replied, "Let anyone among you who is without sin be the first to throw a stone at her." Realizing that they were all sinful, they shamefacedly dropped their stones and left the woman with Jesus. He told her that he did not condemn her, and to "go your way, and from now on do not sin again." (John 8:3–11)

TEACHING THE CROWDS

The Jesus of the Gospels was a gifted teacher. Whether alone with the disciples or in a crowd, he easily fell into the role of teacher. But he did not teach "proper" religious belief and observance of

This illustration of the parable of the adulterous woman is by a seventeenth-century French artist, Nicolas Colombel.

the law. Rather, he was a teacher of wisdom, a guide to greater intimacy with the Jewish God.

As he wandered the countryside, Jesus taught not so much with sermons or lectures as with stories, proverbs, and simple conversation. He used the basic elements of peoples' lives—stories of shepherding and gardening, images of nature. He asked questions to get his hearers to think matters through, and encouraged them to use their imagination and intelligence to see the kingdom of God dawning around them:

THE ANAWIM

A remarkable aspect of Jesus' life was his connection to the anawim, the outcasts of society. In the Jewish belief system of his day, many categories of people were considered unclean and sinful. These people were looked down upon and excluded from making sacrifices at the temple.

Those with diseases were thought to have sinned or to be the children of sinners. The poor and uneducated—often ignorant of religious laws—were considered sinners, as was anyone unable to pay the temple tax. Those in unclean professions, such as gambling or prostitution, were "outside the law" and therefore outside God's saving power.

Tax collectors were particularly despised because they collected Roman taxes and acted as agents of the Romans. Yet according to the Gospels, tax collectors, the poor, the sick, and the sinners, were precisely those to whom Jesus brought the "good news" of God's forgiveness and love: "those who are well have no need of a physician, but those who are sick; I have come to call not the righteous but sinners to repentance." (Luke 5:31–32) Understandably, they were also among those who responded most enthusiastically to Jesus.

Ask, and it will be given you; search, and you will find; knock, and the door will be opened for you. . . . Is there anyone among you who, if your child asks for bread, will give a stone? Or if the child asks for a fish, will give a snake? If you then, who are evil, know how to give good gifts to your children, how much more will your Father in heaven give good things to those who ask him! (Matthew. 7:7–11)

Often, he taught in parables. A parable is a story similar to a fable. It uses simple characters and situations to illustrate a message. Jesus' parables challenged his hearers to see themselves and one another in a new, enlightened way. When he told a lawyer to love his neighbor if he wanted to gain eternal life, the lawyer asked, "Who is my neighbor?" This parable shows Jesus' response:

In reply, Jesus said, "A man was going down from Jerusalem to Jericho, and fell into the hands of robbers, who stripped him, beat him, and went away, leaving him half dead. Now by chance a priest was going down that road; and when he saw, he passed by on the other side. So likewise a Levite . . . passed by on the other side. But a Samaritan while traveling came near him; and when he saw him, he was moved with pity. He went to him and bandaged his wounds, having poured oil and wine on them. Then he put him on his own animal, brought him to an inn, and took care of him. The next day he took out two denarii, gave them to the innkeeper, and said, 'Take care of him; and when I come back, I will

A nineteenth-century illustration of the parable of the Good Samaritan

repay you whatever more you spend.' Which of these three, do you think, was a neighbor to the man who fell into the hands of the robbers?" He said, "The one who showed him mercy." Jesus said to him, "Go and do likewise." (Luke 10:30–37).

Jesus tried to attract people by his healing and through his teachings. Another way he invited people to take part in the kingdom of God was by eating with sinners. This must have been shocking to the "respectable" people. To them, contact with religiously unclean people, especially the intimate act of sharing food, would pollute the righteous. Jesus, a rabbi from a good family, had no business associating with outcasts.

Jesus knew his society's prejudice. By calling people of all stripes—wealthy and poor, righteous and sinners—to share his table, he was making a scandalous statement. He was creating a model of the kingdom of God, showing people that to enter it, they had to put away prejudices. Jesus conveyed this idea in various ways: In the parable of the Good Samaritan, for instance, the Samaritan hero was a member of a despised and "impure" community. Jesus brought a message of healing to the excluded, and a challenge to the excluders.

This theme of the inclusive dinner party as an image of the kingdom runs through the Gospels. Thus, as his followers sought to remember him after his death, their gatherings took the form of a common meal, a "love feast." However, certain religious leaders around Jesus began to take offense at his violation of sacred taboos.

CHAPTER SEVEN

A CHALLENGE TO THE ROMANS

Jesus' message of love and forgiveness seems harmless today. Yet his way of life and his teachings alarmed many in first-century Palestine. Whether accurately or not, both the Romans and the highly placed Jewish leaders in Jerusalem were beginning to be concerned about this "rabble-rousing" Jesus. What was it about Jesus that made enemies as well as devoted followers?

A DANGEROUS REVOLUTIONARY?

Above all else, the Romans were empire builders. Their primary concern was simple: Make sure that conquered peoples stay conquered and continue to pay taxes. The independent Jews of Palestine had been making trouble since the beginning of the Roman occupation in 63 B.C.E. Jewish groups such as the Zealots, often based in the rugged hiding places of Galilee, constantly preached revolution and hatched plots. The Romans reacted by clamping down on anything that looked like trouble; making a example of anyone suspected of being a rebel.

The Romans did not see Jesus as his fellow Jews saw him. They were uninterested in his religious message. They cared only about ending political threats. To them, the crowds around Jesus meant trouble, a potential riot. Anyone stirring the people's passions could have only one thing in mind: revolution.

Was Jesus a revolutionary, bent on liberating the Jewish nation? The question is still debated today. Some of his followers, such as Simon the Zealot, probably thought so. Yet there is no record in the Gospels of Jesus preaching revolution. His message of peace, forgiveness, and love extended even to one's enemies, and it had little room for violence.

Jesus taught his hearers to find creative ways to defeat not one's enemies, but conflict itself. He suggested a better way to deal with enemies— whether Roman or others. For instance, the Roman soldiers forced Jewish citizens to carry their military gear for a mile. A natural reaction to this demand would be to feel humiliation or to lash out in violence. Jesus suggested that a wiser response would be to turn the tables on the soldier: "If anyone forces you to go one mile, go also the second mile." (Matthew 5:41) By freely offering help, one could "disarm" the soldier, who would then wonder whether force really was the only way to relate to the Jews. By appealing to the Romans' humanity, it might be possible to break down the barriers between oppressor and oppressed. The alternative, especially in such a militarily lopsided situation, was death: "All who take the sword shall perish by the sword." (Matthew 26:52)

"All who take the sword shall perish by the sword."

This approach meant neither passive acceptance of Roman rule nor collaboration with the Roman occupiers. Indeed, Jesus disdained both the Roman Empire and those who benefited from their relationship with the occupiers. Instead, he challenged his fellow Jews to create a society of such righteousness that it would transform the world around them, even the Romans themselves. This lofty ideal drew on the centuries-old Jewish belief that they were to be an instrument of God's enlightenment for all other peoples to emulate, "a light to the nations." (Isaiah 49:6)

THE RIDDLE OF THE COIN

One incident reveals another aspect of Jesus' understanding of the Romans. Some religious leaders asked him a simple question, "Is it lawful to pay taxes to the emperor, or not?" They may have been trying to trap Jesus in a "no-win" situation: If he said "no," he would have been guilty of treason against the Romans, a capital offense. But paying taxes to an emperor who claimed to be divine was a violation of the Jewish law, which was built on the idea that there was one God alone.

Jesus' response was typical of his skill as a teacher. Throughout the Gospels, Jesus used the teaching method of answering a question with a question, thus forcing his questioners to think for themselves. Asking for a Roman coin with Caesar's image on it (interestingly, he did not have one), he asked, "Whose head is this, and whose title?" The answer was "the emperor's." Jesus then responded, "Give to the emperor the things that are the emperor's, and to God the things that are God's." (Mark 12:12–17)

"Give to the emperor the things that are the emperor's."

Although there are a number of ways to interpret this riddle-like response, perhaps Jesus was contrasting the kingdom of the Romans with the kingdom of God. Under Roman rule the emperor was worshiped, while the people were exploited and treated with cruelty. The reign of God was dif-

Coins throughout the empire carried an image of the emperor, Julius Caesar.

ferent. The Jews owed allegiance to God, not to an earthly ruler. Jesus may have been saying that it's not the act of paying the taxes that matters so much as one's attitude toward the money. He may have been telling his Jewish listeners to free themselves of the greed and idolatry represented by the coin and by Roman rule, and live instead in God's kingdom of mutual support and love.

Was Jesus' vision of the power of God's kingdom hopelessly optimistic? There are suggestions in the Gospels that some Romans became sympathetic toward Jesus, and there is even a story of Jesus helping a Roman centurion by healing his servant. Acting in love, bridging the gulf between Jew and Roman, Jesus may have influenced some Roman "enemies." Yet if we look at the historical record, his program appears to have failed. He was eliminated, divisions within Jewish society persisted, and continued violent resistance to Roman rule brought exactly what Jesus had feared: utter destruction.

THE MESSIAH?

The Roman rulers of Palestine didn't distinguish between Jesus' program of Jewish self-renewal and the revolutionary plots of the Zealots. They were particularly upset that some Jewish followers of Jesus were calling him "Messiah." As the coming of the Messiah would threaten Roman rule, the Romans came to see Jesus as an enemy. The question remains, however, did Jesus think of himself as the Messiah?

Since his death, it has been taken for granted by Christians that Jesus was the Messiah in some sense. Indeed, the word *christos*, or Christ, is the Greek translation of "Messiah." Yet in the Gospels, Jesus only once spoke of himself as the Messiah. (Mark 14:61–62) More often, he avoided

THE DESTRUCTION OF JERUSALEM

After Jesus' death in about 30 C.E., relations between the Romans and their Jewish subjects continued to deteriorate. In 66 C.E., outright war broke out, and for over four years Jewish revolutionary forces waged a remarkably effective guerrilla war against the powerful Roman troops. Ultimately, however, the might of the empire was too great. After a long siege marked by horrible starvation and disease, the holy city of Jerusalem fell to the Romans in the year 70 C.E.

Thousands of Jews were slaughtered, the city leveled, and the temple destroyed. The remaining Jewish population was taken as slaves or scattered through the countryside. With the destruction of Jerusalem and its great temple, the Jews in a sense endured an apocalypse, but without the great restoration of King David's kingdom that they had hoped for. The tragedy, and the loss of the temple, forced dramatic changes in the development of Judaism from that point onward.

This painting by a seventeenth-century French painter, Nicolas Poussin, shows the destruction of the temple of Jerusalem in 70 C.E.

the subject, perhaps because he didn't want people to pay more attention to his title than to his message. If he did think of himself as the Messiah, it was probably as a different kind of Messiah than most Jews were expecting.

So the evidence for how he thought of himself was unclear from the start. Just as with his "kingdom of God" teachings, Jesus spoke in ways that left plenty of room for listeners to arrive at their own understanding. Perhaps Jesus himself was unsure of his role. As a young man just beginning his ministry, he may have needed more time to understand his part in God's plan.

In any case, attaching a label to his name may not have been as important to Jesus as it was to his followers—or to the Romans. The Gospels show Jesus speaking much less about himself than about God, the kingdom of God, and the path to redemption. And these messages were directed squarely at his fellow Jews, not at the Romans.

CHAPTER EIGHT

A CHALLENGE TO HIS OWN PEOPLE

The Romans weren't the only ones who distrusted Jesus. Many of Palestine's wealthy and powerful citizens felt uneasy about the wandering preacher. Some of the important people of Jerusalem respected Jesus, but many others were offended by him. Here was a rabbi, a teacher of the Law, who seemed to prefer the company of the unclean to that of respectable people like them. He was insulting both their religious standards of purity and their social standards of class distinctions.

What's more, Jesus often preached about how money and power can blind one to one's duties to God and neighbor. This was a time of economic crisis in Palestine. Increasing debt and land-grabbing tactics by the wealthy were creating a class of landless outcasts. Recent studies have revealed that the gap between the rich and the poor was widening in first-century Palestine. This was creating a society badly at odds with the long-standing Jewish ideals of justice and equality.

THE DANGER OF WEALTH

Jesus was sensitive to this problem. His compassion for the powerless combined with his disappointment that the upper classes let this happen to their fellow Jews. To help his society rethink their priorities, he set about to redefine "greatness." It lay, he claimed, not in having riches or high position or great knowledge. True greatness came from humbling oneself and putting others first: "Whoever wishes to be great among you must be your servant, and whoever wishes to be first among you must be your slave, just as the Son of Man came not to be served, but to serve." (Matthew 20:26–27). This greatness, not the false greatness of power and money, would help create the kingdom of God, and it was available to all.

This was a hard message for those who prided themselves on their estates and their importance. Although Jesus did not preach against the wealthy, he did echo the challenges of the earlier Hebrew prophets: Put God and his kingdom first, or you will find yourself disappointed. The reckless pursuit of money can lead one to mistreat one's fellow Jews. It can lead to a miserable state of anxious possessiveness. Trusting too much in riches can mean trusting too little in God's promise to look after his people: "And do not keep striving for what you are to eat and what you are to drink, and do not keep worrying . . . instead, strive for his kingdom, and these things will be given to you as well." (Luke 12:29–31)

A story in the Gospel of Luke reveals Jesus' teaching on the true meaning of abundance. At the beginning of the story Jesus rejects the role of judge. Rather than encourage the legal wrangling between the two brothers, he shows them a better way to avoid conflict in the first place:

> Someone in the crowd said to him, "Teacher, tell my brother to divide the family inheritance with me." But he said to him, "Friend, who set me to be a judge or arbiter over you?" And he said to them, "Take care! Be on your guard against all kinds of greed; for one's life does not consist in the abundance of possessions." (Luke 12:13–15)

A CHALLENGE TO THE RELIGIOUS LEADERSHIP

Another group that probably felt threatened by Jesus was the Jewish leadership itself. The Jewish council, known as the Sanhedrin, consisted of aristocratic Jewish elders and the chief priest, and was led by the high priest, Caiaphas. Under the Romans, the council had limited power, mainly taking responsibility for running the temple, collecting temple taxes, and overseeing the religious life of the Jewish people.

Yet the position of these elders was impossibly tricky, for they had to be intermediaries between the Romans and the Jewish people. The Romans held them responsible for uprisings against Roman rule, saying in effect, "If you can't control your own people, we'll dismiss your council and run everything ourselves." Many Jews, however, saw the Sanhedrin collaborators as more concerned with pleasing the Romans than with looking after the spiritual welfare of the Jewish people.

The Sanhedrin, then, had the unpleasant task of policing their own people, lest the Romans take on the job with much harsher methods. It is in this context that we must see the high priest's wary attitude toward Jesus. Caiaphas worried that Jesus was attracting too many followers, and that this "rabble" would alarm the Romans.

Jesus' teachings probably didn't win him friends among the Jewish leadership, either. The Gospels report his angry accusations against "the Pharisees and scribes." He attacked these educated Jewish teachers as being so concerned with minor laws that they lost sight of the great commandment at the heart of the Law, the love of God and neighbor.

Jesus called the Pharisees and scribes hyp-

A painting by a nineteenth-century French artist, James J. Tissot, shows Jesus rebuking the scribes and the Pharisees.

ocrites for going through the motions of worship but neglecting "the weightier matters of the Law, justice and mercy and faith." (Matthew 23:23) He accused them of creating a barrier to the kingdom of God by separating the Jewish people into "clean" and "unclean," by exalting themselves at the expense of the outcasts. Indeed, the Gospels record more anger on Jesus' part toward these Pharisees and scribes than toward the Romans.

The picture of the Pharisees in the Gospels is not fair, and it is important to understand how biased and incomplete it is. The Pharisees had faults, but were devoted followers of their religion. Their commitment to Judaism, and especially to the Law, kept it alive in the dark years after the destruction of the temple. Why, then, did Jesus condemn the Pharisees?

Scholars tell us that it is unlikely that all these harsh words came from Jesus. Much of the anger toward the Pharisees and scribes actually seems to have come from the Gospel writers. Many Christian communities were beginning to lose their Jewish roots and to see themselves as

PHARISEES AND SCRIBES

Politics and religion in first-century Palestine were inseparable. Just as political parties in the United States argue about the identity and destiny of the American people, the various religious parties in Palestine differed over what made a "good Jew" and what the Jews should do about the Roman occupation.

The Essenes and the Zealots followed a separatist path. Two other groups, the Pharisees and the Sadducees, were more integrated into Jewish society. Neither group was happy about the Roman presence, but had learned to live with it. Both tried to maintain their Jewish identity by sticking strictly to the Law. They differed on topics such as which texts were sacred and if there was life after death. The members of these groups were usually well-educated, well-off male citizens, many of whom were priests, rabbis, and experts in the Law. The term "scribes" refers to these experts in the Law.

following a new and distinct religion. This sometimes led to tension with the established Jewish leaders. Then this hostility probably led the Gospel writers to add their own anti-Pharisee, anti-Jewish feelings to their accounts of Jesus' "sayings," with tragic consequences for Jewish-Christian relations for the next two thousand years.

Yet even allowing for the liberties taken by the Gospel writers, it seems probable that Jesus was frustrated by the hypocrisy of some of the Jewish leaders. Whenever he saw adherence to the Law blinding people to the need for compassion, he spoke out. We see several examples of this when Jesus healed on the Sabbath, an activity forbidden because it was considered work. Jesus' response on one such occasion was, "If one of you has a child or an ox that has fallen into a well, will you not immediately pull it out on a Sabbath day?" (Luke 14:5) From this response, we can gather that while Jesus did not reject the Law, he did reject interpretations of the Law that interfered with doing God's work of caring for the needy.

It is likely that, along with the high priest Caiaphas, certain of the established Jewish priests and rabbis felt threatened by the radical Judaism Jesus was preaching, and by his increasing popularity.

CHAPTER NINE

LAST DAYS IN JERUSALEM

As a devout Jew, Jesus probably made the three- or four-day journey from Galilee to the holy city of Jerusalem many times. He may have traveled there every spring for the festival of Passover, as he did when he was twelve. Passover, Pentecost, and Tabernacles were the three pilgrimage festivals that Jews were expected to celebrate in Jerusalem every year.

During the week leading up to the sacrifices at the temple, Jerusalem's streets swelled with Passover pilgrims from all over Palestine. Thousands more came from the many Jewish communities scattered around the Mediterranean region. Passover carried a political meaning as well as a religious one, for in celebrating the escape from slavery in Egypt, the people were really celebrating their longing for freedom. For the Romans, Passover just meant more unruly Jews to watch over.

ONE LAST JOURNEY

For Jesus, this Passover was different. He had been preaching, teaching, and healing for one to three years (according to the different Gospel accounts). He had attracted enough attention to encourage many in the crowd to expect dramatic action from him, action worthy of the Messiah. At the same time, the Romans (and possibly the Jewish authorities) wondered if they should get rid of him. Why, then, did he decide to leave the security of Galilee and go down to Jerusalem, the center of Roman power and political unrest?

We can't know Jesus' intent as he ventured into the lion's den. The Gospels depict this last trip to Jerusalem as the climax of his career. They show him traveling there with a sense of foreboding, predicting his own death and the destruction of Jerusalem. The Gospel of John pictures him moving across the countryside secretively, to avoid plots against him by the Jewish leadership. This is very likely an exaggeration on John's part, but Jesus probably did realize that he could no longer travel to Jerusalem without attracting large crowds of expectant Jews—and the brutal crowd-control measures of the Romans. Perhaps he saw this Passover as his final chance to appeal to his people for reform, before the Roman dragnet closed in on him.

Whether or not he had a specific plan, Jesus was drawn to Jerusalem, despite the danger. Like the great Hebrew prophets before him, crying out in the streets of Jerusalem, challenging the people of God to make themselves worthy of the name, Jesus may have felt called to bring his message to the heart of the Jewish nation at a time when the city would be filled with Jews from every corner of the empire. And so, in April of the year 30, with his disciples, "he set his face to go to Jerusalem," (Luke 9:51) ready for whatever his prophetic mission would bring him.

When Jesus entered Jerusalem, the Gospels tell us, he was welcomed by cheering crowds, hailing him as "the one who comes in the name of the Lord—the king of Israel!" (John 12:13) Yet in the days to follow, Jesus did not act like a "king of Israel." He did not confront the Romans, nor did he rally the crowds to revolt. Rather, he stepped up his challenge to the people to reform themselves, their society, and their religion.

"The one who comes in the name of the Lord—the king of Israel!"

Teaching the crowds in the gathering places of Jerusalem, Jesus condemned the hypocrisy of the "scribes and Pharisees." He spoke of the commandment to love God and neighbor, and told parables of the coming of the kingdom. Many of his teachings were about the need to prepare oneself by rejecting the values of Caesar's kingdom and embracing the values of God's kingdom.

"CLEANSING THE TEMPLE"

The story of the "cleansing of the temple" reveals the energy Jesus brought to his final week in Jerusalem. The temple, the holiest site in

The "cleansing of the temple," as Jesus drove out the traders, was depicted by the painter El Greco, about 1600.

Judaism, was also a busy marketplace. Passover pilgrims changed their Roman or foreign currency into special temple coins, and then purchased pigeons and animals for sacrifice. This flourishing trade at the edges of the temple was accepted, for it made possible the important priestly sacrifices within. Yet it offended Jesus, and in a dramatic act, he "entered the temple of God and drove out all who were selling and buying in the temple." (Matthew 21:12)

What exactly he was protesting is still debated. The temple had long been a source of controversy. The taxes that kept it running were a burden to the peasantry and enriched the priestly class. The animal sacrifices, some said, distracted the people from their obligation to God: "Cease to do evil, learn to do good, seek justice, rescue the oppressed, defend the orphan, plead for the widow." (Isaiah 1:16–17) Jesus may have been echoing the harsh words and dramatic actions of earlier prophets, as he

> **"Cease to do evil, learn to do good, seek justice."**

cried out, "It is written, 'my house shall be a house of prayer,' but you have made it a den of robbers." (Luke 19:45–46) To Jesus, the buying and selling at the temple may have represented how his beloved religion had become corrupted by greed and exploitation, the values of the kingdom of Caesar.

No police action seems to have followed Jesus' outburst. Scholars point out that the temple was too huge for one man to clear. Perhaps the protest was more symbolic than the Gospels suggest, hardly enough to bring the police. In any case, for several days after, Jesus apparently continued to teach in and around the temple. The incident was enough, however, to seal his fate.

EYEWITNESS ACCOUNTS?

Each of the Gospels devotes about a third of its story to the final week of Jesus' life—known as "the Passion" (from a Latin word meaning "to suffer"). Clearly, the Gospel writers considered this the crucial time—the climax—of Jesus' life and career.

And yet even these richly detailed accounts leave us asking many questions. The first should probably be: "How reliable are they?" For the Gospels themselves tell us that when Jesus was arrested, his disciples and friends "deserted him and fled." (Mark 14:50) Who, then, was left to witness the trials, torture, and execution that rapidly followed Jesus' arrest? Even if an eyewitness had remained, it is unlikely that the authorities would have allowed him or her to attend the trials where Jesus' fate was determined.

Most scholars today agree that many of the

details of the Passion are less historical fact than "imaginative retelling" by the Gospel writers. Building their stories on rumors and educated guesses, the writers re-created the scene to give greater drama and meaning to the basic story.

What can we really know about Jesus' final days? The scholars tell us we can be almost certain of the following: Jesus was executed by crucifixion in Jerusalem, during Passover, under the authority of the Roman governor, Pontius Pilate. The year was probably 30 C.E. The rest is silence . . . or perhaps not. The Passion accounts in the Gospels contain enough clues to give us a sense of what might have happened in those last hours. What follows, then, is an investigation into the possibilities, an attempt to sort out what is probable from what is unlikely.

A PLOT?

The first thing that strikes one about the timing of Jesus' arrest is that according to the Gospels, it took place several days after his outburst in the temple. Between the outburst and the arrest, Jesus moved about Jerusalem freely, leaving the crowded city in the evening with his disciples to sleep in the nearby countryside, and returning in the morning. Yet the Romans liked to move swiftly. If they had considered him a real threat, they probably would have arrested him on the spot, rather than allowing him to stir up the crowds for several more days. What changed their minds about Jesus? What convinced them that this wandering preacher was more than just an idealistic dreamer, that he was in fact a dangerous revolutionary?

Nobody disputes that the Romans passed the sentence on Jesus and executed him as a political threat to the empire. Yet there is the charge in the Gospels that the Jewish authorities had a role in it as well. The Gospels tell how the chief priests and elders of the Sanhedrin council met to plot Jesus' arrest and execution. They are said to have "feared the people." (Luke 22:2) That means they worried that the Jewish crowds were getting carried away in their enthusiasm for Jesus as the Messiah. John tells of high priest Caiaphas' argument that unless Jesus was eliminated, the crowds would become so unruly that the Romans might become alarmed and crack down hard on all Jerusalem. (John 18:14)

As the Gospels report, the council members decided to arrest Jesus and deliver him to the Romans, to protect public order (and perhaps the Sanhedrin's own position of power). Unable under Roman law to carry out a political execution themselves, they would try to convince Pilate that Jesus was a dangerous rebel and should be killed. The arrest itself would have to happen in a quiet place, away from the crowds, who might riot if they knew their "Messiah" was being taken from them.

The Gospels tell the story well. Yet there are several reasons to question the notion of a Jewish plot. First, how could the Gospel writers have learned the details of the plot? Plots are, by definition, secretive, and the Sanhedrin would certainly have kept their plans to themselves.

More importantly, we must remember that the Gospel writers composed their stories at least forty years later. This was a time of great hostility between the followers of Jesus, now called "Christians," and the leaders of mainstream Judaism. Most scholars agree that this hostility led the Gospel writers to unjustly blame the Jews for Jesus' death, just as they had pictured Jesus as harshly attacking the Pharisees. This anti-Jewish sentiment, written into the Passion story, was thus preserved and resulted in a belief that "the Jews killed Jesus." More than just a harmful misconception, this incorrect belief has resulted in 1,900 years of hostility toward and persecution of the Jewish people. Only in this century, with the coming of responsible biblical scholarship, is this poisonous misbelief fading.

So the Romans, not the Jews, killed Jesus. Still, scholars are divided over whether the Sanhedrin encouraged the Romans to take action. The Jewish authorities had reasons to wish to be rid of Jesus. This would explain Jesus' delayed arrest. The Sanhedrin may have decided after the temple incident that Jesus had gone too far, and they may have discussed ways to convince the Romans to get rid of him. If there was a plot, it was in motion within a few days, by the end of Passover week.

THE LAST SUPPER

What were Jesus and his disciples doing while his fate was being decided in Jerusalem's halls of power? We know that he spent time that week teaching, perhaps healing, and criticizing certain rabbis and priests. Whether the crowds were really starting to see him as the Messiah is another unanswered question. We know more about his enemies' view of him than about what he and his followers thought was happening.

There is one episode, however, in which we get a glimpse into his followers' private world. Jesus gathers his disciples for a Passover meal that becomes their "last supper" together before Jesus' death. Perhaps Jesus sensed that he had pushed the authorities too far; that the end was near, and he wanted to make this meal special. The traditional Christian notion of what happened at the meal is that Jesus offered his body and blood, in the form of bread and wine, as a sacrifice for his people, thus initiating the Christian ritual known as the Eucharist. Although this may be a retelling crafted by later Christian writers, it is not unlikely that Jesus asked his disciples to remember him when they broke bread together after he was gone.

From the meal, the Gospels tell us, Jesus and the disciples retreated to rest and pray at the Mount of Olives, a quiet olive grove outside the walls of Jerusalem. One of the twelve disciples, though, was not with them. Judas had struck a bargain with the Sanhedrin. In exchange for thirty pieces of silver, he would lead them to a place where Jesus could be arrested without interfer-

The Last Supper, *by the Florentine artist Leonardo da Vinci (1452–1519)*

ence from the crowds. There on the Mount of Olives, in the dark and quiet of the night, he came with the troops to arrest Jesus.

The betrayal by Judas may be another imaginative detail added by the Gospel writers. One way or another, though, Jesus was arrested, either by Roman soldiers or by the Jewish temple police, and hauled away to prison. It was at this point that the disciples, in fear for their lives, fled.

TRIAL

According to the Gospel accounts, Jesus was hustled early the next morning through a series of quick and seemingly pre-determined trials. In a trial before Caiaphas and the Sanhedrin, Jesus was judged guilty of blasphemy, that is, falsely declaring himself the son of God. The "evidence" for this charge came either from false witnesses or misinterpretations of Jesus' teachings. Although he may have called himself the son of God, most scholars do not think he was saying that he had a unique relationship to God, but that he, like everybody, was one of God's children.

Interestingly, Jesus did not defend himself. His response in this trial and in the later trial by Pilate was either silence or "you say that I am." This fits with Jesus' apparent preference for letting others make up their minds about him, rather than making pronouncements about himself. Then, too, he may have understood that his death had already been decided; these trials were a formality and it was pointless to try to defend himself.

"You say that I am."

From the Sanhedrin trial he was taken to Pilate, to be tried as an enemy of Rome. Pilate would not have cared whether or not Jesus called himself "the son of God," but agreed to execute Jesus. What we know of Pilate suggests that he would not have hesitated to condemn a Jewish troublemaker. Like so many other "rebels," Jesus would be crucified as a warning to future troublemakers.

CRUCIFIXION

After the trial, nothing was left but to carry out the sentence. Within a few hours of his arrest, Jesus was on the way to the public execution site called Golgotha. There he was bound or nailed to the cross, and left to hang, while the Roman guards idly awaited his death. Sometimes, a crucifixion victim's sentence was written on a board and nailed to the cross so that horrified onlookers would know what crimes to avoid. To Jesus' cross was attached the half-mocking, half-warning title "Jesus of Nazareth, King of the Jews."

While in custody, Jesus had been mocked, tormented, and flogged by Roman and Jewish

A depiction of Jesus appearing before Pontius Pilate, based on a painting by Michael Munkacsy, a nineteenth-century painter from the Austro-Hungarian Empire

guards. In a weakened state, he died quickly. Crucifixion victims sometimes lived for days, but the Gospels say that Jesus hung on the cross for half a day, from mid-morning to mid-afternoon, dying at last with a loud cry.

Jesus' male disciples had long since fled. It was up to the female disciples and relatives to take down the body. These women were safe because the Romans generally didn't see women as potential rebels. They buried Jesus in a nearby tomb, unlike most crucifixion victims, who were tossed into a shallow grave. He was about thirty-three years old at his death.

Thus ended Jesus' life, in seeming failure and humiliation. The crowds who had hailed him as their king had given up on him, and his dream of a new Israel—built on repentance, justice, and love—was, it seemed, forgotten.

CRUCIFIXION

One of the keys to the Romans' success in conquest was their use of brutal methods. Although earlier groups, including the Assyrians and the Persians, practiced crucifixion, the Romans perfected its use as a warning. In their hands, crucifixion was not just another form of execution; it was a public spectacle of humiliation, torture, and agonizing death. Rebellious slaves, prisoners of war, and political rebels were its primary victims, for these were the groups to whom the Romans wanted to send a clear message: "Oppose Rome, and this is what will happen to you."

The ordeal of the condemned criminal began with a public beating. He would be stripped naked and whipped with metal- or bone-tipped leather lashes. He would then be forced to carry the crossbeam of his crucifix to the public execution site outside the city walls. There he was strapped or nailed to the wooden cross, and left to hang for as long as it took to die. Exposed to the elements, weakened by his wounds and by thirst, the victim would eventually die of suffocation. As his body collapsed, so did his lungs. It was indeed, as the Jewish historian Josephus said, "the most wretched of deaths."

The scene of the crucifixion, as drawn by
Hans Holbein, a German artist (1497–1543)

CHAPTER TEN

The life of Jesus was extraordinary in many respects. Perhaps strangest is that, according to the Gospels and to Christian believers, his greatest achievement occurred after death. The Gospel accounts state that after three days in the tomb, Jesus returned to life and rose from his grave. Appearing to his followers, he comforted and instructed them, and after forty days among them, he ascended into heaven.

Each Gospel recounts the story of the resurrection somewhat differently. Other, non-biblical accounts vary as well, suggesting that different groups of Christians understood the resurrection in different ways. The "official," Christian view of his resurrection message is best expressed in the Gospel of Matthew, which has the risen Jesus tell the astonished disciples:

All authority in heaven and on earth has been given to me. Go therefore and make disciples of all nations, baptizing them in the name of the Father and of the Son and of the Holy Spirit, and teaching them to obey everything that I have commanded you. And remember, I am with you always, to the end of the age. (Matthew 28:18–20)

Whatever happened in the days following Jesus' execution, the resurrection is a story that belongs more to the world of belief and faith than to strict historical biography. The historian can say little about it except that somehow, sometime after his death, an experience of Jesus' presence was felt by his followers. This experience transformed them from scared and scattered fugitives into confident, joyous groups of believers, boldly proclaiming the life and message of Jesus the Christ.

MAKING SENSE OF JESUS' DEATH

What did these earliest Christians believe, and why were they now calling him Jesus the Christ? Scholars think that the followers of Jesus probably first went through a period of shock and despair at the loss of their beloved leader. Then they did what any Jew would have done: they searched the scriptures to try to make sense of the tragedy.

In the Hebrew Scriptures, they found passages

A ninth-century miniature depicts Matthew composing his gospel account of the life of Jesus.

that convinced them that maybe Jesus was not a failure: maybe he was the Messiah after all. They found passages such as Isaiah 52:13–53:12 that speak of a "suffering servant" sent by God, who is "despised and rejected" by those he has been sent to save. They found Psalms that depict God's servant suffering violence at the hands of evil people. And they found predictions such as that of the prophet Hosea, who claims in 6:2 that "on the third day, he will raise us up, that we may live before him." These passages and others suggested to Jesus' followers that it was part of God's plan all along to have Jesus suffer, die, and be resurrected on the third day.

A "suffering servant"

Slowly, they came to believe that their Messiah was not the kind who would lead the Jews to victory over the Romans. Rather, he was the suffering servant promised in the scriptures, who would be brought low and then raised up to bring them strength and inspiration. This Messiah (*christos* in Greek), they believed, was now a living presence among them, their lord and master. He had freed them from the burden of their sins by taking upon his own shoulders all the sins of the world. He had shown them the way to live in harmony and love in this world. By defeating death, he had opened to them the possibility of eternal life in the world beyond. They came to believe that his "kingdom of God" was yet to come, and that he would return in glory to usher it in. This mix of Jesus' earthly teachings, Jewish belief in the apocalypse ("the end-time"), and the early

Christians' interpretation of the meaning of Jesus' death eventually formed the core of Christian belief.

THE FIRST CHRISTIANS

Until Jesus' final coming, when he would judge the world and welcome only the righteous into his kingdom, his followers felt a responsibility to spread "the good news" about Jesus to everyone. And so begins the story of the early Church, the first small bands of Christians who, though still Jewish, began a movement that in time would become a distinct religion. In the decades following Jesus' death, these earliest Christians committed themselves to living out Jesus' teachings and bringing his message to the world.

For this story, we have some good sources. The New Testament's "Book of Acts," which describes the actions of his first-century followers as they spread through the eastern Mediterranean region, is a wealth of information. Later writings also give us an idea how these earliest Christians lived and worshiped.

We know, for instance, that these first Christians all followed the Jewish laws and worshiped in the Jewish temple and synagogues. Most were Jewish by birth, while some were gentile (non-Jewish) converts to Judaism who then became attracted to the sect of Jesus-followers. Through the first century, the Christians saw themselves as Jews with a special Messiah, whose message of social justice and eternal life gave them special hope. They tried to follow his example and his teachings by sharing their possessions, eating together in fellowship, caring for the sick and troubled, and giving what they could to the poor.

Indeed, many of them were from the poorer classes themselves. They were probably impressed by the tales they heard of Jesus' healings and his love for the lowliest among them. Slaves, outcasts, impoverished widows and orphans, as well as some wealthy citizens, were all drawn by the warm sense of community, equality, and mutual support demonstrated by the Christians.

Following the lead of Jesus himself, the earliest Christian groups seem to have offered women greater acceptance, freedom, and equality than was common at the time. Until well into the second century, when Church leaders began to assert male control over the Church, we find women playing prominent roles in many Christian communities. Women acted as ministers, prophets, teachers, missionaries, and martyrs. Many non-biblical accounts give great honor to the female disciples, especially Mary Magdalene, and to later female saints such as Perpetua and Felicity, who were killed for their beliefs by the Romans in the North African city of Carthage.

In the decades following Jesus' death, early Christians were not always well received by their fellow Jews. Most Jews did not believe that Jesus was the Messiah. Many felt that the Christians were weakening the Jewish religion by preaching an "alternative" Judaism. Jewish leaders hostile to Jesus and his followers had hoped that his movement would die with him. When they saw that groups of Christians were springing up and spreading, they became alarmed and may have tried to arrest some of the Christian leaders.

Tensions grew between mainstream Judaism and the new Christians. By late in the first century, Christian communities were losing their Jewish identity, and the Jewish leadership was excluding them from worship in the synagogues. The first converts to Christianity usually came from the Jewish population but, with time, Christian missionaries began welcoming gentile converts as well. These gentile converts, with their non-Jewish beliefs and ways of life, brought changes to the Christian communities. These changes became so far-reaching that the Christian movement could no longer call itself a Jewish sect. Christianity had become a religion of its own.

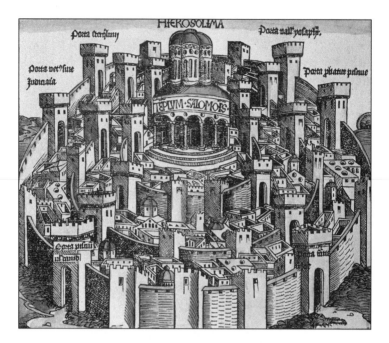

*A fifteenth-century woodcut shows the
walled city of Jerusalem.*

OUTSIDER ACCOUNTS OF THE
FIRST CHRISTIANS

As Christianity spread and asserted its identity, it
drew more attention from non-Christian writers.
These "outsider" reports, though few, are valuable
to the historian. Since non-Christians had no rea-
son to make up a character called "Jesus," these
accounts are strong evidence that Jesus was a

real person, and not just an invention of the Gospel writers. These non-Christian historians and public officials were reporting events that were widely known at the time.

Josephus, writing between 90 and 100 C.E., gives us the first and most important of these reports:

> At this time there appeared Jesus, a wise man. For he was a doer of startling deeds, a teacher of people who receive the truth with pleasure. And he gained a following both among many Jews and among many of Greek origin. And when Pilate, because of an accusation made by the leading men among us, condemned him to the cross, those who had loved him previously did not cease to do so. And until this very day the tribe of Christians, named after him, has not died out. (Antiquities 18.3.3)

Other writers less friendly toward the "tribe" of Christians have also left us scraps of information. A Roman governor of Bithynia (in what is now Turkey), in the early second century described the practices of the local Christians and wondered whether he should punish them as a sect hostile to the rule of Rome. The second-century Roman historian Tacitus described how

"Christus" suffered execution under Pontius Pilate, and how a "deadly superstition" sprang up in his name, spreading from Palestine to Rome.

These reports are valuable not just as supporting evidence for some of the Gospel claims about Jesus, but also for what they tell us of how outsiders saw the Christians. Prejudice against Christianity, such as that expressed by Tacitus, led to the Roman persecution of Christians until early in the fourth century.

A MAN CALLED SAUL

One of these outsiders became Christianity's most famous convert, and helped change Christianity forever. At the time of Jesus' death, Saul of Tarsus was a Jewish rabbi and Pharisee. He was hostile to the young Christian movement, and determined to help destroy it. When he learned that the Christians had spread to the city of Damascus (capital of present-day Syria), he set out from Jerusalem to stop them. On the way, according to the Book of Acts, he was knocked to the ground and blinded by a vision of Jesus. In a dramatic conversion, he took the name Paul and turned his tremendous energies from fighting Christianity to promoting it.

Paul devoted the rest of his days to spreading "the good news," God's promise of salvation through the crucified and resurrected Jesus Christ. He was convinced that Jesus' saving power belonged not only to the Jews, but to all peoples, and he helped convince the Christian leadership in Jerusalem to allow gentile converts. Like some of Jesus' original twelve disciples, he traveled throughout the eastern Mediterranean region on dangerous missionary journeys. Everywhere he went, he and his small band of helpers tried to convert people to the Christian faith.

Spreading "the good news"

Paul often encountered opposition to his vigorous preaching, and was frequently run out of town for challenging the local gods. Yet he was successful in starting many new communities of converts. Several of the letters he wrote to these fledgling Christian communities were such powerful statements of Christian belief and living that they were included in the New Testament.

Paul was executed around 65 C.E., one of many victims of anti-Christian persecution ordered by the crazed Roman emperor, Nero. By the time of his death, Paul had helped transform the Christian movement. From a weak Jewish splinter group in Jerusalem, it had become a network of linked communities spread through the eastern Mediterranean region. By his preaching

*The Dutch artist Rembrandt van Rijn (1606–1669)
portrayed Paul in prison awaiting execution.*

and letters, Paul had helped transform Christian belief as well. In Paul's theology, the man Jesus became "the Christ," a universal, godlike savior for all. And by writing in Greek, the common written language at the time, Paul, along with the Gospel writers, laid foundations for the universal religion that Christianity was to become.

DIVISIONS AMONG CHRISTIANS

In the centuries following Jesus' death, Christians everywhere tried to follow his teachings on love and brotherhood. Yet they disagreed on certain questions. Who was Jesus really? Was he just a man, or God, or the Son of God, or a spirit? Which were his most important teachings? Which accounts should be accepted and which rejected? Who should lead the growing Church? These and other questions plagued Christians for centuries, resulting in some sharp divisions and even bloodshed.

The story of the growth and spread of Christianity is long and complex. It is a story of men and women struggling to live out their faith. It is the story of how the teachings of a first-century Jewish rabbi became one of the most widespread religions in the world. And it is the story, sadly, of how his teachings were frequently twisted or ignored to serve some people's desires for wealth and power. But that is a story for another book to unravel.

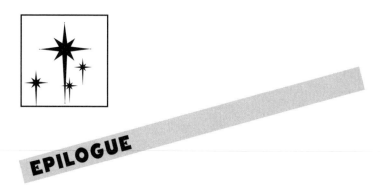

What, then, do we really know about the man Jesus of Nazareth? Most biblical scholars contend that we can state few facts with confidence: Jesus was born in Palestine toward the end of the reign of Herod the Great (37 to 4 B.C.E.). He was linked to John the Baptist before becoming a wandering religious teacher with disciples, and he was executed by the Romans during the reign of Pontius Pilate (26 to 36 C.E.). The rest is educated guesswork: attempts to reconstruct his life not with certainty but with varying degrees of probability. Through this work, biblical scholars have arrived at some important insights.

Yet many Christians stress that gaining insight into the life of Jesus is not the only way to "know" Jesus. Jesus enters the lives of Christian believers less through historical scholarship than through faith in the man revealed in the Gospels.

This man is more than just a man—he is the bridge between the world of ordinary human beings and the world of the spirit. For Christians who experience him in this way, he becomes, in a way mysterious but real, a transforming presence, a source of ongoing hope and inspiration, a glimpse into the divine.

Some Christians criticize the work of biblical scholars. They claim that historical research undermines Christian faith by representing Jesus as just a man, or by denying that Jesus existed. Yet this is not the objective of today's researchers, many of whom are believing Christians. By enlightening our understanding of Jesus, their work can contribute to, not destroy, the faith of Christians. The scholars' findings offer benefits to Christians and non-Christians. As examples, here are two practical contributions to our world that historical research has made:

Clearing up misconceptions. In the past two thousand years, many horrible deeds have been committed in the name of Jesus. The more accurate a picture we have of the historical Jesus, the more clear it is that such deeds are contrary to his life and teachings. An example of this is the notion that "the Jews killed Jesus." Biblical scholarship has shown this to be false. As more people think historically and understand the profound Jewishness of Jesus, the long tradition of bigotry toward the Jews should, one hopes, fade away.

Contributing to deeper spiritual insight. For many people, Christian and non-Christian alike, the image of Jesus in traditional Christian churches is that of a stern and sin-obsessed ruler. This image, a product of centuries of misunderstanding of the historical record, has made it hard to see Jesus for who he really was. Recovering the original Jesus through historical scholarship has helped many to grasp and experience his gentler message of God's unconditional love.

An example of such a transformation in the life of a Christian is that of John Shelby Spong, the Episcopal bishop of Newark, New Jersey. Bishop Spong grew up in a church with a narrow, unhistorical understanding of Jesus. Like many Christians through the ages, the members of this Christian church imagined Jesus as a heavenly judge quick to condemn all those considered "sinners." When he went to college and seminary, Bishop Spong began to understand that the historical Jesus was less interested in judging people than in breaking down the barriers that divide them. Understanding this made Bishop Spong want to do the same, and as a church leader, he has worked to make his church as welcoming and inclusive as possible.

Bishop Spong's study of the historical Jesus has helped him arrive at a more mature appreciation of Jesus and a deeper faith. The following excerpt from one of his books gives his vision of who Jesus was, and who Jesus is:

A man named Jesus of Nazareth had lived among them. He had a unique capacity to be. His gift was to be whole, free, and giving, which in turn seemed to cause those around him to live fully and more completely. He seemed to have an infinite capacity to love, to forgive, and to accept others. He appeared to enhance the personhood of every human being who touched his life. . . . Women, Samaritans, gentiles, lepers, those judged to be unclean felt his touch and were called into a new dignity. . . . He had the capacity to live in the present moment, to drink from that moment all of its wonder, to scale its heights and to plumb its depths, to enable that moment to share in eternity.

CHRONOLOGY

37–4 B.C.E.	Herod the Great rules Palestine under the Romans
27 B.C.E.–14 C.E.	Reign of Augustus, Roman Emperor
c. 4 B.C.E.	Birth of Jesus
14–37 C.E.	Reign of Tiberias, Roman Emperor
26–36	Pontius Pilate rules Judea as Roman governor (procurator)
27	Baptism of Jesus by John
c. 27–30	Jesus' Ministry
30	Jesus goes to Jerusalem
c. 30	Crucifixion of Jesus

Apocalypse—the end of the present age, when some believe that God will destroy the world as we know it and bring about a new age of glory for the righteous. Apocalypticism is the Jewish or Christian belief in this event.

Apostle—another term for "disciple," a follower of Jesus: used also to refer to other important early Christian missionaries.

Bible—the Bible is the holy book of both Jews and Christians. The Hebrew Scriptures (sometimes called "the Old Testament") consist of the Torah (Law), the Prophets, and the Writings (assorted scriptures including the Psalms and the Book of Job). The Christian "New Testament" consists of the four Gospels, the Book of Acts, Paul's letters, several other letters, and the Book of Revelation.

Christ—a Greek word meaning "the Messiah."

Church—"the Church" is the term used to refer to the collection of all early Christian communities throughout the Mediterranean region. These individual churches were usually led by priests or deacons; churches in a large area were overseen by a bishop.

Essene—a member of a radical Jewish sect in Jesus' day. The Essenes lived a desert life of ritual purity in preparation for a bloody apocalypse.

Eucharist—the Christian commemoration of the Last Supper and celebration of Christ's presence.

Gentile—a person not of the Jewish faith.

Gospel—Old English for "good news." A biography-like report of Jesus' life, written by an early Christian. The Bible contains four Gospels—Matthew, Mark, Luke, and John.

Mediterranean region—those lands bordering the Mediterranean Sea.

Messiah—a Hebrew word meaning "the anointed one." A special king and savior expected by the Jews to bring about a new and glorious age for the Jews and for all humankind.

Orthodox—literally, "correct belief." Conforming to the official doctrine and belief held by the established institution within a religion, *e.g.* orthodox Christianity, orthodox Islam.

Palestine—the ancient homeland of the Jews, present-day Israel.

Passover—one of the holiest periods in the Jewish calendar, marking the deliverance of the Jews from oppression in Egypt.

Pharisees—a group of Jews in Jesus' time and afterwards, committed to the strict observance of the law.

Roman Empire—the most powerful empire in Jesus' time. The Romans ruled all of Palestine, as well as much of the rest of the Mediterranean region, extending all the way to present-day Britain.

Resurrection—the Christian belief that Jesus rose bodily from the tomb after three days.

Scribe—an educated expert in the Jewish Law; also, one whose job is to copy and transmit sacred texts.

Synagogue—a gathering place of prayer and religious learning for the Jewish people.

Zealot—a member of a group of Jewish radicals devoted to the military overthrow of Roman rule.

A NOTE ON SOURCES

With the recent increase in historical research into the life of Jesus, there is no shortage of sources on the topic. Works I have found particularly useful and insightful are these: *Jesus: A New Vision* by Marcus Borg (Harper and Row, 1987); *The Essential Jesus: What Jesus Really Taught* by Dominic Crossan (HarperCollins, 1995); *The Message and the Kingdom: How Jesus and Paul Ignited a Revolution and Transformed the Ancient World* by Richard A. Horsely and Neil Asher Silberman (Putnam Books, 1997); *The Real Jesus* by Luke Timothy Johnson (HarperCollins, 1997); *The Gospel According to Jesus* by Stephen Mitchell (Harper Perennial, 1993); *Gospel Truth* by Russell Shorto (Riverhead Books, 1997); and *Born of a Woman* by John Shelby Spong (Harper, 1992).

FOR MORE INFORMATION

BOOKS

A good place to start any study of the life of Jesus is the Bible, particularly Isaiah, Samuel, the four Gospels, and the Letters of Paul.

Batchelor, Mary. *Opening Up the Bible*. Elgin, Illinois: Lion Publishing, 1993.

Bishop, Clair Hutchet. *Yesu, Called Jesus*. An appealing historical re-creation of what Jesus' early years may have been like.

Borg, Marcus. *A New Vision*. San Francisco: Harper and Row, 1987. A vivid picture of the life of Jesus in a cultural and historical setting.

Hoffman, Yair. *The World of the Bible for Young Readers*. New York: Viking Kestrel, 1989.

Mitchell, Stephen. *The Gospel According to Jesus*. New York: Harper Perennial, 1993. An insightful look at Jesus as a spiritual master;

recommended for those interested in parallels between Jesus' teachings and those of other spiritual traditions.

Shorto, Russell. *Gospel Truth*. New York: Riverhead Books, 1997. An excellent survey of recent findings and controversies about Jesus.

INTERNET SITES

Many Internet websites deal with the life of Jesus. Yet only a few contain reliable, scholarly information on the historical Jesus. These are some of the best, and easiest to use.

Frontline: From Jesus to Christ: The First Christians
http://www.pbs.org/wgbh/pages/frontline/ shows/religion
A visual and text guide to historical information about the life of Jesus and the rise of Christianity.

The Jesus Seminar Forum
http://religion.rutgers.edu/jseminar
A website devoted to research, study, and debate about the historical Jesus.

Into His Own: Perspectives on the World of Jesus
http://religion.rutgers.edu/iho
This site is a tool for the study of Christian scriptures and the history of Jesus and his world.

INDEX

ABOUT THE AUTHOR

Ramsay M. Harik is a writer and teacher from Bloomington, Indiana. He studied at Princeton University and Indiana University, and earned a Master of Theological Studies from Harvard Divinity School. He has taught in Beirut, Lebanon; in Virginia, and as a Peace Corps volunteer in Cameroon; and has lived and traveled in several Middle Eastern countries. His previous book for Franklin Watts, *Women in the Middle East: Tradition and Change*, was published in 1996. He currently teaches religion at the Academy of the Sacred Heart in New Orleans, Louisiana.